05.60

P4c

Names and Descriptions

Logic

1 2 3 1

2 A C

LEONARD LINSKY

Names and Descriptions

⅃L

The University of Chicago Press
Chicago and London

The University of Chicago Press, Chicago 60637
The University of Chicago Press, Ltd., London

© 1977 by The University of Chicago
All rights reserved. Published 1977
Phoenix Edition 1980
Printed in the United States of America

81 80   9 8 7 6 5 4 3 2

Library of Congress Cataloging in Publication Data

Linsky, Leonard.
Names and descriptions.

Bibliography: p.
Includes index.
1. Reference (Philosophy)   2. Names.   3 Description
(Philosophy)   4. Modality (Logic)   5. Semantics
(Philosophy)   I. Title.
B105.R25L56   110   76–8093
ISBN 0–226–48442–4 (paper)

To Joanie

Ich hätte gerne ein gutes Buch hervorgebracht.
Wittgenstein

Contents

Preface

This work continues the studies in the theory of reference presented in my *Referring* (London: Routledge and Kegan Paul, 1967). I remember one day in Oxford, many years ago, when Gilbert Ryle said to me that one reason for publishing a book is that it enables one to get free of a subject; to move on to other things. It was then certainly my intention to turn to other matters, and Ryle's words were a spur. But I could not put the subject aside. For one thing, as soon as my book appeared there were parts I came to dislike in it, so I kept on thinking about the topics in an attempt at least to satisfy myself. Later I was convinced that the book contained mistakes and I wished publicly to correct them. On the other hand, in the years since the publication of *Referring* there have appeared works by others on the same and related topics. This too stimulated me to reconsider my views and to think about matters which had not before concerned me, or which had not seemed problematic. Stimulation from this source came mainly from the published lectures of Saul Kripke. His work has revolutionized the subjects with which it deals and it renders much previous work out of date. Serious further research on these topics must deal with Kripke's contribution. A great deal of what I have written here is a response to it. Indeed, had it not taken account of Kripke's views, I could not have expected this book to be of interest to present-day readers. And were it not for this stimulus, I probably would not have been motivated to write it.

I have been at work on this book for a long time. One consequence is that some redundancy and repetition have crept in. When I began, sometimes after a long interruption, to write again, I could not always keep in mind everything I had already written over this long period. I was able to remove some repetition in the final stages of my work, but not all of it. Some I wanted to retain, when it was a matter of arriving at the same (or nearly the same) topics or conclusions in different ways and from different starting points. Then at last, the effort of continual reworking was too great. I have had to content myself with what I knew I could improve, if the work I had already done was not to be wasted—if the book was ever to be published. I wanted to free myself of it.

A lot of what is here has been learned from others. I have already said something of what I owe to Saul Kripke. My debt to Michael Dummett's monumental work on Frege is equally great. It was from Dummett that I learned to appreciate the importance of Frege's concept of sense as a *cognitive* concept, its role in an account of what we know when we know the meaning of a word or sentence. I have devoted a good deal of part I of this book to the attempt to show that Kripke's arguments do not force us to abandon Frege's concept in its application to proper names. Any reader of Dummett's great work will see its influence on me at these places and elsewhere in the first part of my book. Help has also come from my students at the University of Chicago to whom all of the material contained here was presented on several occasions in different versions. Among these students there has always been a small, especially interested group which has repeatedly corrected errors and stimulated my thinking. I would like especially to mention Bob Richardson and Jack Snapper. My colleague Bill Tait listened to me and helped when I fumbled with some of the logical niceties involved in this work. He helped me to see mistakes and to improve formulations, and he encouraged me. It is especially gratifying to acknowledge a debt to my son Bernard Linsky who read parts of the work and discussed them with me. His dissertation on natural kinds has influenced my thought on this topic. My wife Joan was of great help on questions of style.

Some of the book was written in Florence during the autumn of 1974. I found an ideal setting in which to write at the *Istituto Nazionale Di Studi Sul Rinascimento* in the imposing Palazzo Strozzi. The directors generously overlooked the fact that my work had nothing to do with the Renaissance and allowed me to use their *sala* as a place in which to write.

I owe a more personal debt to the Bartolini family in Florence, Genni and Tina. They have, for many years, provided a warm and friendly home for me in Italy overlooking the Arno at the magnificent Ponte Santa Trinita. This atmosphere of friendliness in the midst of great beauty is an inspiration to achievement. At least, I felt it.

Chicago–Florence

Introduction

The subject of this book is singular reference; proper names and definite descriptions. The discussions which follow continually center around several puzzles. They puzzled Meinong, Frege, and Russell, the founders of the modern theory of reference. These philosophers shaped their theories with one or more of the puzzles in mind and they designed their theories to deal with them. In this book the views of these philosophers and others will be constantly before us and always with the aim of first determining and then critically evaluating the solutions they have to offer to our puzzles. If it were not for the puzzles, singular reference would not be a topic of philosophical interest. They arise in the attempt to understand the logic of statements about existence, necessity, identity, and belief, as these statements involve singular terms.

The first of our puzzles is about reference and existence. What is the logical form of negative existential sentences such as 'Pegasus does not exist'? In a sentence such as 'Socrates is a Greek', the name 'Socrates' stands for an object and the rest of the sentence denotes a property which the sentence attributes to him. And that sentence is true just in case the object named by its grammatical subject *does* have the property which is attributed to it. There is no alternative to this account, barring ontological qualms about properties as opposed to classes. The logical form of 'Socrates is a Greek' is transparent. But nothing like this account will do for 'Pegasus does not exist', for, to begin with, we cannot apparently even take 'Pegasus', the grammatical subject of the sentence, as standing for an object. What object? Are there objects which do not exist (are not)? The classical theory of quantification avoids the problem by not allowing individual constants which lack denotation. The problem is not, however, to devise some technical change in classical logic to fill this gap, but to give a theory of proper names which takes seriously the fact that they can and do sometimes denote things which do not exist. Any adequate theory of reference will have to do this. This is the subject of part I of this book.

In this first part, I present, discuss, criticize, and evaluate theories of several philosophers about reference and existence. I deal with theories of Mill, Russell, Frege, Searle, Meinong, Wittgenstein, and Kripke. I do not offer another theory of my own. This is not because I agree with Wittgenstein's view that there is no place for theories or explanations in philosophy. Nor is it because I agree with Kripke that because philosophical theories are all false we should stop making them. My way of proceeding with this topic is to examine the alternative views, to see where each is right and wrong and why. My method is to test the theories by confronting them with the puzzles. But those puzzles which are of central importance for some authors move to the fringe or drop out of sight entirely for others. So when an author has produced a theory which does not deal explicitly with one of our puzzles, I undertake to fill the gap myself, that is, to show how the principles involved in the theory implicitly allow an application to the novel material. In some cases that cannot be done and I take that as a mark against the theory. My assumption is that the best theory (or theories) will solve all the puzzles in the best way. By this criterion none of these views emerges as totally adequate and none clearly superior to the others. Each emphasizes important considerations which are ignored by the others. But typically, a theory is developed by taking certain facts, cases, and puzzles as central and others are allowed to take care of themselves, provision having been made for the central cases. What is central varies from theory to theory. What is ignored often does not fare too well.

The result of a detailed and careful study of these theories should be a more nearly adequate view of the terrain which concerns us. Only my readers can decide how far I succeed in this. It is always my aim to come to a conclusion after a problem has been raised or a view discussed. The reader will not be left in doubt about what I think about the matters I discuss and why I believe what I do. In this way I do, after all, present my own theory.

The problem about negative singular existential sentences naturally divides into two parts according to whether the singular term involved is a proper name or a definite description. (In Russell's view there is just one problem here, but that involves a very substantial theoretical claim.) Chapters 1 and 5 deal with the problem as it concerns proper names, while chapter 2 deals largely with definite descriptions. The first chapter is introductory, providing historical background for the discussions of part I. Chapter 3 discusses the concept of rigid designation. Although both proper names and descriptions are discussed, I deal mostly with proper names in this part. This is because what is needed now is a corrective to the established logical tradition which concentrates on descriptions while either leaving ordinary proper names pretty much without special treatment (Frege) or assimilating them as truncated or disguised descriptions as a matter of theory (Russell).

Meinong's theory of objects made central the problem of singular reference and existence. Frege's starting point is with a puzzle about singular terms and identity. Identity is a relation which holds between objects, but only between an object and itself. How then can an identity-statement, $a=b$, tell us anything other than just that $a=a$, if $a=b$ is true? Yet there are statements of identity which convey important additions to our knowledge. 'Venus=the morning star' is Frege's famous example. It was the attempt to deal with this problem which led Frege to make his distinction between the sense and reference of a term.

As I proceed in these chapters, confronting the theories with the puzzles, I often argue that in designing a theory to deal with one or more puzzle, an author has either neglected to apply his theory to other puzzles or has fallen into difficulties as great as

Introduction

those he has attempted to overcome by making an application
of his theory to the other puzzles about reference impossible, very
difficult, or strained and unintuitive. In the discussions of part I,
a single issue about proper names emerges as the center around
which the rest revolves. Do proper names have sense (connotation) or only denotation? John Stuart Mill held the view that
proper names have denotation without having connotation. The
tradition originating with Russell and Frege, the founders of
modern logic, holds that they have connotation as well. For
Frege this idea takes the form that proper names have both
sense and reference. For Russell the idea takes the form that
proper names are abbreviations for descriptions. Kripke advocates the abandonment of this logical tradition and a return
to Mill's view. His arguments divide into two groups. One set of
arguments turns on the logical behavior of proper names in contexts governed by the modal concepts of necessity and possibility;
mainly identity-contexts. These arguments aim to show that the
logical behavior of proper names in modal contexts is radically
different from that of definite descriptions. If these arguments
are sound, they refute Russell's theory that names are truncated
descriptions. These modal arguments are the topic of chapter 3.
The other group of Kripke's arguments against the description
theory of names concerns the analysis of negative existential
statements. In chapter 5, I deal with these arguments. The fifth
chapter also discusses an alternative to the description theory put
forth by Kripke and Donnellan, the causal theory of names; and
an alternative analysis of negative existentials suggested by the
causal theory. The central issue about connotation and denotation of proper names takes the form of the adequacy of the description theory in these chapters. In chapter 4, I argue that
Kripke should not have rejected Frege's notion of sense as
applied to both singular terms (such a sense Carnap called an
"individual concept") and to names of natural kinds. I argue that
the sense theory is compatible with the thesis that names are
rigid designators.

The second part of this book is about reference and modality.
'Socrates is a Greek' has a transparent semantical analysis of a

xviii

kind which cannot be extended to 'Pegasus does not exist'. This is the source of the problem of reference and existence. The obvious account of the first sentence is seen further to be inapplicable to such a sentence as 'Nine is necessarily greater than seven'. We cannot here just take 'nine' to name an object which is ascribed the property of being necessarily greater than seven. For if it were, the sentence 'The number of the planets is necessarily greater than seven' should also be true. Does it not ascribe the same property to the same object? Nine *is* the number of planets. But the first sentence is true and the second apparently is not. Apparently a rose by any other name does not *necessarily* smell the same. The same phenomenon arises with sentences expressive of propositional attitudes, such as belief. A person may believe that nine is greater than seven and yet not believe that the number of the planets is as well. But if 'nine' is not just a name for a subject of predicates in these sentences, what is it doing there? How must the obvious semantical account of 'Nine is greater than seven' be modified to deal with the modalized embeddings of this sentence?

This problem is sometimes cast in another form. The classical semantical analysis of sentences turns on an intimate interrelation of quantifiers and singular terms. Indeed to be a singular term is, in this analysis, simply and solely to be a substitute for a bound variable. So if 'nine' is just a name for a subject of attributes in 'Nine is necessarily greater than seven' we should, by existential generalization, be able to quantify it out to obtain the sentence 'Something is necessarily greater than seven'. But this last seems to lack a clear sense, for what is it which is supposed to be necessarily greater than seven? Nine, of course! But that is the number of the planets which, according to the doctrine of necessity, lacks this attribute. We are apparently in a muddle. The difficulty is reproduced in the case of sentences expressive of propositional attitudes, such as belief.

It was W. V. Quine who first urged these difficulties in the form presented in the last paragraph. They were for him reason enough to abandon the whole project of quantified modal logic in both the narrow sense of logical necessity and the broader sense of the propositional attitudes. Over the years, nothing has proved to be a stronger stimulus to the development of these subjects than the attempt to refute, or otherwise undercut, Quine's attack upon their legitimacy. Now, I believe, the dust of controversy has settled. It is time to take stock; to decide who was right and who was wrong and to see what can be learned from this lengthy, often very confused and complex, but enormously enlightening discussion. This is my aim in the second part of the book.

Chapter 6 presents Quine's attack on modal logic, as well as the case of those who find Quine's arguments vitiated by inattention to the scope ambiguities induced by definite descriptions in modal contexts. I argue that each side in this dispute can reasonably find the other begging the main question. The main question, as Quine saw, is essentialism. Chapter 7 presents Kripke's formal semantics for quantified modal logic. I want to show where, in a precise formal account, the issue of essentialism surfaces. Confusions have appeared here too. One confusion is the issue about the criteria of identity for individuals across possible worlds. This, I argue, is a pseudoproblem, though essentialism in other forms is a genuine issue which remains to be confronted in the new context. I argue for the intelligibility of a modest version of this doctrine. At the end there is a chapter on substitutional quantification where the main problems of the book are considered from the point of view of this interpretation of quantifiers. Because the chapter does not fit squarely into either part of the book, and also because some of it digresses from the main issues altogether, it has been placed as an appendix to the rest.

The problems of the book have a common center. They are about logical form. In each case a certain classical logical analysis is seen to have its limitations. This classical analysis is entirely adequate and without a rival within its domain of application. The problems arise because of the limitations of this domain. It does not include negative singular existentials such as 'Pegasus does not exist', and modal statements such as 'Nine is necessarily greater than seven' or 'George IV believes that Scott

Introduction

is the author of *Waverley*'. Our puzzles can all be seen as arising from an attempt to force these sentences into the classical mold. This is, I believe, the source of the difficulties. Our sentences cannot fit the mold. The problem is to find alternatives. A great deal of the best philosophy of this century has been devoted to this task. It is the subject matter of that branch of philosophy which is now called "philosophical logic."

The problem of accounting for the logical form of our puzzle-sentences represents one major trend in the philosophical work of our time. It continues the program which Frege initiated in his *Begriffsschrift* of 1879. This program should be seen in contrast with those contemporary discussions which stem from Wittgenstein's later work with their emphasis upon the study of the regularities governing our *use* of language. Here the problem of logical form has no place, though it dominated Wittgenstein's earlier philosophy contained in the *Tractatus Logico-Philosophicus*. This book was a work in the Fregean tradition. It is this that marks the real difference between Wittgenstein's early and late philosophical standpoints. The later philosophy turns away from the problem of logical form. It studies the criteria for the correct use of a word or sentence without raising the issue of the semantical analysis of the internal structure of different kinds of statements. It has long been my view that both kinds of work are valuable and worthwhile in the philosophy of language, and in this book I have attempted to bring both currents together where it seemed that there was a genuine advance in our understanding in doing so.

Reference and Existence

1

Existence and Proper Names

This chapter states the problems and presents the recent historical background of the discussions of part I of this work.

Russell says of the purported name 'Romulus', "If it were really a name the question of existence could not arise. . . ."[1] In *Principia Mathematica* Russell sought to realize this idea in the requirement that the quasi predicate of singular existence (E!) must be attached to definite descriptions and never to proper names (individual constants or individual variables) as subjects. E!(a) and E!(x) and their "negations" are not well formed. But Russell was wrong about *Principia* on this, since it does provide a way of saying what he regarded as in violation of correct logical grammar; the sentence $(\exists x)(x=a)$ says what Russell says cannot be said, namely, that a exists.

That both 'a exists' and 'a does not exist' are meaningless (where 'a' is a proper name) Russell thought a consequence of his theory of naming. According to this theory the meaning of a proper name is its denotation. Hence if 'a does not exist' is true it contains a meaningless subject term. On the plausible assumption that if one term of a sentence is meaningless, the whole sentence is as well, Russell arrived at the paradoxical conclusion that these purported assertions can only be true if meaningless.[2] If true singular negative existentials are meaningless, so are their positive counterparts, for mere negation cannot transform a meaningful assertion into nonsense.

The careful reader will have spotted the fallacy. It lies in "the plausible assumption" that if one term of a sentence is meaning-

3

less so is the entire sentence containing it. This is not plausible but absurd if the only sense in which the relevant term is "meaningless" is that it lacks a denotation. The whole argument could be put to better use to show that it is wrong to identify the meaning of a term with its denotation. Certainly the argument does not show the meaninglessness of existentials of the form $(\exists x)(x=a)$ and $\sim(\exists x)(x=a)$ which serve quite well, up to a point, in place of the forms which Russell proscribed. The point at which they fail comes with the matter of truth, for in the language of *Principia* all negative existentials of this kind are false. *Principia*'s implicit semantics excludes nondenoting (vacuous) proper names. (The theorems of *specification*, $(x)\varphi x . \supset . \varphi a,$ and *existential generalization*, $\varphi a . \supset . (\exists x)\varphi x,$ just say that every individual constant denotes.) So we reject Russell's argument to show that 'a does not exist' is meaningless, if true. We have claimed that *Principia* does not meet Russell's requirement that both positive and negative singular existence assertions always involve definite descriptions and never proper names, but it must be admitted that *Principia* is in harmony with Russell's intuition that there is something paradoxical about true negative existentials involving proper names. In *Principia,* $\sim(\exists x)(x=a)$ is false for any choice of individual constant in place of 'a'.

Rejecting Russell's argument that 'a does not exist' is meaningless, if true, does not require us to reject his view that the meaning of a proper name is its denotation. This is a premiss for his argument and is a fundamental principle of his theory of proper names; and so far we have no reason to reject it. We are left with the question of whether there are any logically proper names in ordinary language. And, of course, we are still in a position to argue against Russell that it is rather a deficiency of *Principia* that we cannot say in it, 'Santa Claus does not exist'. In saying of 'Romulus' that if it were really a name the question of existence "could not arise," Russell clearly intended the implication that since "the question of existence" can arise, 'Romulus' is not really (logically) a name. But, of course, 'Romulus' is a paradigm case of a name from the point of view of its surface grammar. Russell's theory is that it and all ordinary proper names, from the point of view of a correct logical analysis of their functioning, are disguised definite descriptions, thus not logically names, despite the appearance of their surface grammar. A principal argument for this view is the fallacious one just given. We can sensibly question the historical reality (existence) of Romulus, and we can intelligibly conclude that Romulus did not exist. Since '*a* does not exist' is nonsense if '*a*' is logically a name, it follows, by this argument, that 'Romulus' is not logically a name.

Frege had earlier advanced the theory that proper names have both sense and reference. According to Frege, the relation of denotation in which a singular term stands to its referent is routed through the sense of that term. Singular terms *express* a sense which is a *concept of* a unique object. The relative product (in the sense of relation-algebra) of the first of these relations into the second is the relation of *denotation* in which the singular term stands to that object of which the sense which it expresses is a concept. Frege's analysis of denotation requires the route through sense.

We can now briefly compare and contrast Russell and Frege on the relation between ordinary proper names and definite descriptions. According to Russell, these names are "disguised" or "truncated" descriptions. It is thus that true singular negative existentials are possible, for we have seen that Russell held that '*a* does not exist' is always either false or lacking in meaning if '*a*' is logically a name. Thus if someone asserts 'Santa Claus does not exist' we must first determine which definite description the name replaces before we can determine the content of their assertion.

Frege never says anything explicitly about the analysis of negative existentials involving proper names, but it is possible to construct a Fregean position from his explicitly stated views. First, we have Frege's principle that if a constituent name of a complex name lacks a referent, so does the whole complex name containing it. Second, we have Frege's principle that (declarative) sentences are complex names whose referents are their truth-values. Frege says, illustrating these principles, "The sentence 'Odysseus was set ashore at Ithaca while sound asleep' obviously has sense. But since it is doubtful whether the name 'Odysseus', occurring therein, has reference, it is also doubtful whether the whole sentence has one."[3] It would seem to follow from these two principles that every (declarative) sentence containing a nondenoting name lacks a truth-value, and hence that 'Pegasus does not exist' is not true but truth-valueless. But Frege can, I think, be rescued from this paradox. There is another Fregean principle according to which names in oblique contexts have as their referents what in an ordinary context is their sense. Thus, since negative singular existentials involving proper names do have truth-values, it follows that 'exists' in these sentences induces an oblique context in which the proper name denotes its customary sense.

For Frege, names are not truncated descriptions. They sometimes, as in singular negative existentials, denote their customary sense rather than their customary referent. Sometimes a definite description does have the same sense (at least for some users of the language) as some proper name. Frege gives explicit examples of this.[4] These descriptions can replace the proper names whose sense they express without altering the sense of any complex name containing these proper names. But it would be a great mistake to think that, according to Frege, the sense of *every* proper name is identical with that of some definite description. Kripke regards Frege as committed to the description theory of names (all proper names are disguised descriptions) only because he holds the sense theory (proper names have sense), but Frege does not hold the description theory. This matter will be taken up again in chapter 4. I only want to indicate here that there is no reason to believe that the sense theory of proper names entails the description theory. Frege accepts the former and not the latter.

While Frege does not hold that ordinary proper names are disguised descriptions as Russell does, he would agree with Russell that the logical behavior of proper names is the same as that of definite descriptions. For this reason, he called both kinds of singular terms "*eigenname*." But his theory of descriptions was different from that of Russell. Frege requires all singular terms in his *Begriffsschrift* to have a denotation, while Russell allows for vacuous descriptions, though not for vacuous proper names. So there was no need for Frege to single out from his broad class of "proper names" a special subclass of those which are logically guaranteed a referent as Russell does under the name "logically proper names." Further, once all descriptions are accorded a denotation they become freely substitutable for other proper names and they no longer induce scope ambiguities in extensional contexts. For all of these reasons, the logical behavior of descriptions is, for Frege, indistinguishable from that of (denoting) proper names. Russell, allowing for vacuous descriptions, could not freely substitute them for his proper names and had to acknowledge ambiguities of scope for descriptions in *Principia.* He thus was led to distinguish a special class of singular terms, the logically proper names, as logically different in their behavior from descriptions. When it is said that both Russell and Frege treat ordinary proper names as descriptions, these differences must not be forgotten. But they are not of prime importance for our present purposes, so with this caveat, we will continue to refer to the "Russell-Frege" view when the common feature we have in mind is that according to both theories ordinary proper names have meaning.

The Russell-Frege view has not been accepted by all philosophers. Proper names seem to be words having reference without having sense. For this reason it is natural to think of them as not belonging to particular natural languages at all. Would anyone say that 'George Washington' is a couple of English words? At any rate there is a traditional philosophical theory of names beginning with Mill's *Logic* which is built on this intuition. Mill held that proper names have denotation but do not have connotation. (We will not need, for our purposes, to distinguish connotation, meaning, and sense.) As far as this part of his theory is concerned, Russell is a disciple of his godfather. The intuition on which the theory rests is very strong. We do not learn who George Washington is in the course of learning the meanings of English words. Indeed, the question "What does

'George Washington' mean?" is itself meaningless. What is wanted is an answer to the entirely different question, 'Who is George Washington?' This is not a question about the meanings of words but about the denotation of a name. This name plainly does not have a meaning.

If, with Frege, denotation is held to be required to be routed through sense, ordinary proper names present a problem. Even if one is convinced that they must have sense, it is unlikely that they have the same sense for all of their users. (Or in Russell's account: It is not the case that the description which abbreviates the name for one of its users will abbreviate it for all of them.) Both Frege and Russell tried to deal with this problem. They held that while a proper name may have one sense for a given speaker (abbreviate one description for him) it will (in general) not have that sense (abbreviate that description) for another; but it does not matter if a speaker and hearer differ in these ways provided only that the reference of the terms is the same for both. This will assure that the sentence spoken has the same truth-value for speaker and hearer, though, of course, it may express different propositions for each.

(There is a difficulty here which Frege never seems to have faced. He held that in indirect discourse the reference of a name is its customary sense. So if speaker and hearer attach different customary senses to a given name used in indirect discourse, the sentences using this name may express propositions differing even in truth-value for them in spite of the fact that the relevant name has the same customary reference for both.)

The classical philosophical tradition in the theory of reference thus presents us with two opposed views about ordinary proper names. Russell and Frege, the founders of modern logic, represent one view, and Mill the other. Mill's view is that logically a proper name's business is solely to denote its referent; it means or connotes nothing. More cautiously we should say (keeping in mind those names, for example, 'Smith', which do have a meaning) that whatever semantical content or syntactic structure a proper name has is, according to a theory such as Mill's, logically irrelevant to its being a name and functioning as such. This is the point of the tired joke that the Holy Roman Empire was neither holy, nor Roman, nor an empire. All that is required of a sound of our language to be a name is that it be pronounceable and that it purport to have a referent. Any syntactic structure it may have is logically of no significance, and any associated semantic content it may possess is perhaps in some ways exploitable, but still logically irrelevant. The most corrupt of Popes can bear the name 'Innocent' without anyone having made a logical mistake on that account alone. What a name contributes to the truth-conditions of propositions containing it is just the indication of its referent. Mill says, "When we name a child by the name 'Paul' or a dog by the name of 'Caesar', these names are simply marks, used to enable those individuals to be made subjects of discourse."[5]

Russell, like Frege, offers an analysis of naming. It involves the relation of acquaintance. If '*a*' is logically a name for us, we must be acquainted with its denotation. He says its meaning *is* its denotation. He might, I think, as well have stated his position as being that names do not have meaning, only denotation. Of course ordinary proper names generally do not satisfy this requirement. None of us is acquainted with Romulus. So here is another reason 'Romulus' cannot be, for Russell, logically a name. Frege did not hold that names are disguises for descriptions. For Frege names contribute to the senses of the declarative sentences containing them by themselves expressing their senses. The sense of the name conveys information about its referent. This information, together with that contributed by the sense of the remaining parts of the sentence containing the name, determines the truth-conditions for the whole. One who understands the sentence knows how the world must be if it is to be true, for in grasping the senses of the contained names we learn what objects to investigate in order to determine whether or not the world lives up to these truth-conditions. In both Russell's and Frege's view and that of Mill, the business of names is to indicate (name, denote, present, "go proxy for") their denotations. Russell says that names present their denotations to us by our being acquainted with their bearers, and Frege says they do this by expressing a sense which gives a one-sided illumination of their referents. Russell, then, straddles the two positions, agreeing with Mill on those names which for him are logically proper names, and with Frege on ordinary proper names. One might say that, for Frege, ordinary proper names are also logically quite in order.

Kripke criticizes Frege's concept of sense because he says that it runs two notions together: the notion of fixing a meaning and the notion of fixing a reference.

> Frege should be criticized for using the term 'sense' in two senses. For he takes the sense of a designator to be its meaning; and he also takes it to be the way its reference is determined. Identifying the two he supposes that both are given by definite descriptions. Ultimately, I will reject this second supposition too; but even were it right, I reject the first. A description may be used as synonymous with a designator, or it may be used to fix its reference. The two Fregean senses of 'sense' correspond to two senses of 'definition' in ordinary parlance. They should be carefully distinguished.[6]

Certainly a distinction can and should be drawn between fixing the meaning of a singular term and fixing its reference. But Kripke is criticizing Frege for confusing these. He talks of "the two Fregean senses of 'sense'." There is no justification for this attribution. Frege's view is that the fixing of the referent of a term is determined by the fixing of its sense. Reference is routed through sense so that, though the fixing of reference is different from the determination of sense, they are not logically independent of each other. Kripke rejects this view about ordinary proper names. His arguments will be discussed in later chapters. Here I wish to point out only that Kripke has not shown that Frege has two concepts of sense, or that he confuses two concepts of sense. Even if Kripke's arguments show that the sense of an ordinary proper name does not determine its reference, he has not shown this for *all* singular terms, for all that Kripke says against Frege's treatment of proper names leaves unaffected his treatment of other singular terms in terms of the concepts of sense and reference and of the logical dependence between these.

Kripke places a good deal of emphasis on the distinction between fixing the meaning and fixing the reference of designators because he believes that a failure to keep the distinction clear is partly responsible for the description theory of names. According to that theory, names are just disguised descriptions. This is a mistake, he believes, and it was easier to make because the descriptions which fix the references of names were thought to be fixing their meaning (or sense) as well. Kripke's view is that names do not have sense so that the fixing of reference cannot be the fixing of sense. Consider the class of true identities of the form $a=(\imath x)\,(\varphi x)$, where '$a$' stands for an unspecified name. In terms of Frege's concepts we can say in the case of all of these that the referent of 'a' and the referent of $(\imath x)\,(\varphi x)$ are identical. Only in some cases the two terms express the same sense as well. Kripke's point is that any of these true identities may be thought of as fixing the referent of 'a'; all that is required is a coreferential description. But unless the sense of the name is already fixed, the identity itself will lack sense. Let us suppose that 'a' is being *given* a sense with the form of words " 'a' denotes $(\imath x)\,(\varphi x)$." Here Kripke would insist that what is being fixed is the referent of the name, but I cannot see how that is done without fixing its sense. A fuller discussion of this topic will be given in chapter 4. Here I would warn against making the simple mistake of thinking that because the two terms of a true identity may differ in sense, it follows that it is possible to fix the referent of a name without fixing its sense. Kripke, I believe, has made this mistake.

Russell says of an ordinary proper name such as 'Aristotle' that it is not logically a name. He has several reasons. The first is that only thus can we accommodate the fact that the question of the historical reality (existence) of Aristotle can intelligibly arise. If 'Aristotle' is a disguised description, say 'the teacher of Alexander', then the question of the historicity of Aristotle is just the question of the existence of Alexander's teacher. This is a clear question. According to the only alternative account which

Russell contemplates, namely, that the meaning of a proper name is its denotation, proper names do not have senses; the question of the existence of Aristotle (supposing 'Aristotle' to be a name) cannot arise.

Since it is perfectly obvious to us that 'Aristotle' is a name, and that the question of his historical reality can arise, we have no alternative but to reject Russell's view that the meaning of a name is its referent. As far as I know, Mill never acknowledges the existence of a difficulty about this. Yet the problem is as great for him as it is for Russell. If 'Aristotle' has denotation but not connotation, what can be at issue, for Mill, if it is asked 'Did Aristotle exist?' What is at issue if we ask 'Does Santa Claus exist?' Suppose we ask 'Was Aristotle a teacher?' According to Mill's view the sense of the question is clear. In order to answer it we must determine whether the denotation of 'Aristotle', the man, had the property of being a teacher. But an analogous account will obviously not do for our question about the existence of Aristotle. In fact, Mill's theory provides no way of dealing with this difficulty. This puts it at a distinct disadvantage as an alternative to Russell's and Frege's account. More generally, Mill offers no account of vacuous (nondenoting) proper names. Is it his view that 'Santa Claus' has denotation but not connotation, and is simply a mark used to enable that individual "to be made a subject of discourse"? But here there is no individual.

Russell's theory was motivated by a central concern with the problem of negative existentials. Frege, on the other hand, seems never to have been troubled by this issue. He introduces his distinction between the sense and reference of names in order to solve a problem about identity-statements. Is identity a relation? A relation between objects or between names or signs of objects? In his first book, *Begriffsschrift,* he had taken the latter alternative according to which the information contained in an identity $a=b$ is just that 'a' and 'b' are names for the same object.

The reasons which seem to favor this are the following: $a=a,$ and $a=b$ are obviously statements of differing cognitive value; $a=a$ holds *a priori,* and according to Kant is to be labeled analytic, while statements of the form $a=b$ often contain valuable extensions of our knowledge and cannot be established *a priori*. . . . Now if we were to regard equality as a relation between that which the names 'a' and 'b' designate, it would seem that $a=b$ could not differ from $a=a$ (i.e., provided $a=b$ is true). A relation would thereby be expressed of a thing to itself, and indeed one in which each thing stands to itself but to no other thing. What is intended to be said by '$a=b$' seems to be that the signs or names 'a' and 'b' designate the same thing, so that those signs themselves would be under discussion; a relation between them would be asserted.[7]

So Frege's first account had seemed forced on him by the attempt to show how identity-statements could be both true and informative. By the time he wrote "On Sense and Reference," it was clear to him that the earlier solution would not work.

(1) Venus = the morning star
does not just mean,
(2) 'Venus' and 'the morning star' denote the same object (in English).

"In that case," he now objects, "the sentence $a=b$ would no longer refer to the subject matter, but only to its mode of designation; we would express no proper knowledge by its means. . . . If the sign 'a' is distinguished from the sign 'b' only as object (here by means of its shape, not as a sign, i.e., not by the manner in which it designates something), the cognitive value of $a=a$ becomes essentially equal to that of $a=b$, provided $a=b$ is true."[8]

Frege's argument is that all that (2) tells us is that two marks have the same denotation; they are names of the same thing. One who does not know what that denotation is, is told nothing about astronomy by (2). On the other hand, (1) does express an important astronomical fact. So Frege concludes, "A difference can arise only if the difference between the signs corresponds to a difference in the mode of presentation of that which is designated."[9] The sense of a name is just this mode of presentation of its referent.

For Russell, $a=b$ does have the same meaning as $a=a$ if 'a' and 'b' are logically proper names (and if $a=b$ is true). So, Russell concludes that whenever an identity is informative, at least one of its terms is not logically a proper name, but an explicit or disguised description. Thus informative identities are not logically really identities but the generalized statements which result from the elimination of the description(s), in accordance with his theory.

In contrast to both Frege and Russell, Mill's account of proper names as marks having denotation but not connotation, which serve to make their referents subjects of discourse, leaves him unable to explain the cognitive difference between 'Hesperus= Phosphorus' and 'Hesperus=Hesperus'; and 'Cicero=Tully' and 'Cicero=Cicero'. So the very strong intuition that Mill's view is correct runs into difficulties as soon as we try to apply it toward the solution of traditional difficulties about proper names.

Before Russell presented his theory in 1905 in "On Denoting," he had already published an earlier theory in *The Principles of Mathematics* of 1903. It is entirely different in spirit from the later view and much closer to Meinong's theory, which in Russell's subsequent work appears as a paradigm of how not to philosophize about these topics. In the *Principles,* Russell said,

> Being is that which belongs to every conceivable term, to every possible object of thought—in short to everything that can possibly occur in any proposition, true or false, and to all such propositions themselves. Being belongs to whatever can be counted. If A be any term that can be counted as one, it is plain that A is something, and therefore that A is. 'A is not' must always be either false or meaningless. For if A were nothing, it could not be said to be; 'A is not' implies that there is a term A whose being is denied, and hence that A is. Thus unless 'A is not' be an empty sound, it must be false—whatever A may be, it certainly is. Numbers, the Homeric gods, relations, chimeras and four-dimensional spaces all have being, for if they were not entities of a kind, we would make no propositions about them. Thus, being is a general attribute of everything, and to mention anything is to show that it is.[10]

14

So '*A* is not', according to this theory, is always either false or meaningless. It is meaningless if '*A*' denotes nothing, and hence is not a "term" at all. Russell goes on to explain that *existence* is not to be confused with *being,* hence '*A* does not exist' can be true, provided that *A* has being but does not exist. Notice how much of this early theory is retained in the later one. If '*A* is not' is meaningless, it is because '*A*' is not genuinely a term; that is, because it lacks a denotation. The genuine terms of this early theory of the *Principles* become the logically proper names of the later theory. On the other hand, if '*A* is not' is true, it must be because '*A*' is not genuinely a term in spite of superficial appearances. The conclusion is near to hand that the grammatical form misrepresents the true logical form of this sentence and that '*A*' is a disguise for something which is not logically a term at all, just because it denotes nothing.

Russell's early theory of *The Principles of Mathematics* was in the tradition of Brentano and Meinong. One of the tasks Brentano set for himself was to find some characteristic or distinguishing mark which separates psychological or mental acts from physical acts. He discovered this characteristic in "intentionality," a peculiar kind of directedness toward objects. If one sees, one sees something; if one hears, smells, tastes, one hears, smells, or tastes some object. Further, if one opines, supposes, knows, or believes, one opines, supposes, knows, or believes something, some object or other. So all mental acts have objects on which they are directed. In this they differ from physical acts. I can look for an honest man, even if none exists, but I cannot hang an honest man under this condition. So another way of putting Brentano's thesis is to say that psychological or mental acts can be directed toward nonexistent objects but physical acts cannot. This "directedness" of psychical acts is seen as constituting their "intentionality," which means just their characteristic of referring to some object; reference is the peculiar mark of the mental. Meinong, as a disciple of Brentano, formulated his theory of reference around two principal theses: (A) There are objects which do not exist. (B) An object can have properties even though it neither exists nor subsists. As a theory about singular

15

terms in general and proper names in particular, Meinong's view is that all such terms have denotations, that not all of these denotations are (according to (A)) among objects which exist. Further, these terms all denote the "right" object. 'Napoleon' denotes Napoleon, 'Santa Claus' denotes Santa Claus, 'the golden mountain' denotes the golden mountain. For 'the golden mountain' to denote the "right" object it must denote something which is a mountain and is golden. These properties belong to the golden mountain, in accordance with the second thesis, in spite of the fact that this mountain does not exist. So Meinong provides a solution to Russell's puzzle about how it is possible for a negative singular existential such as 'Pegasus does not exist' to be both significant and true. This theory is very much like Russell's own earlier theory of the *Principles*. It is remarkably difficult to refute. Russell thought the theory inconsistent, but his arguments can be answered. This matter will be explored further in the next chapter. Here I am content to have presented some philosophical problems of referring to the nonexistent, of existence and proper names, and to have briefly noticed some of the main theories devised to deal with the problems.

There is an interesting parallel between the development of the theory of reference and the development of set-theory in this century. Cantor's original theory had an immediate simplicity and intuitiveness because it was based upon one powerful and intuitive principle about set existence, the unrestricted comprehension principle, according to which every condition determines the set of just those objects which satisfy that condition. The theory of sets based on this principle originated by Cantor and axiomatized by Frege was shown to be untenable by Russell's discovery of the contradiction called "Russell's paradox." The subsequent history of set-theory has consisted in the development of alternatives to Cantor's original naive view. Several workable alternatives have been explored, but all of them deviate from Cantor's intuitive and simple unrestricted principles of set comprehension. The parallel I have in mind is this. In the theory of reference there is also an intuitive and naive theory which Russell claims to have shown leads to contradiction. Most of the principles of this theory were explicitly adopted by Meinong. The subsequent theories of Russell, Frege, and Kripke all oppose in one way or another the original naive theory. This is why the consideration of puzzles about reference has played such an important role in this subsequent development. This can be made clearer if we first state the naive theory of reference and then show how each of the puzzles challenges one or another of its principles.

This theory is the naive theory of reference in the sense that each of its principles is supported by strong intuitions about the logic of singular terms. These principles, with some examples, are the following:

1. Every purported singular term denotes an object. ('Napoleon' denotes Napoleon.)
2. Some singular terms denote objects which do not exist. ('Santa Claus' denotes Santa Claus.)
3. The object denoted by a singular term is the "right" object. ('The author of *Waverley*' denotes the author of *Waverley*.)
4. An object can have properties though it does not exist. (Pegasus has wings.)
5. The reference of a complex term is a function of the references of its constituent terms. (The denotation of the result of replacing '*x*' by 'France' in 'the capital of *x*' is Paris.)
6. Two terms of a true statement of identity are inter-substitutive *salva veritate*.
7. The sense of a complex term is a function of the senses of its constituent terms.
8. Proper names have denotation but not connotation.
9. There are true identity-statements which are informative.

Russell's puzzle about 'Pegasus does not exist' challenges (1), (2), and (3). In the course of solving this puzzle he was led to deny all of these as well as (4). The puzzle about nine and the number of planets challenges (5) and (6). Frege's puzzle about identity-statements which are both true and informative challenges (8) and (9). No one has formulated a theory which both solves all of the known puzzles and which does not abandon many of the principles of the naive theory and which also is free of difficulties of its own.

2

Vacuous Singular Terms

In *Principia Mathematica* and elsewhere, Russell distinguishes incomplete symbols from logically proper names. Incomplete symbols require "definition in use" because they have no "meaning in isolation." 'Socrates' he says, "stands for a certain man, and therefore has a meaning by itself, without the need of any context."[1] A definite description such as 'the round square' is unlike a proper name in that it does not stand for (denote, refer to, mean) an object at all, for there is no such thing as the round square. (It did not occur to Russell that an improper description such as 'the round square' might still stand for something other than the round square.) Russell gave an argument for this. 'The round square does not exist' is a true proposition. "Yet we cannot regard it as denying the existence of a certain object called 'the round square'. If there were such an object, it would exist: we cannot first assume that there is a certain object, and then proceed to deny that there is such an object."[2] Here is an argument to show that definite descriptions are incomplete symbols; that they do not stand for (denote, refer to, mean) objects. Since propositions containing improper (empty, vacuous) definite descriptions as subjects are sometimes true and hence meaningful, the embedded definite description cannot stand in any semantical relation to the object described, for these propositions would contain meaningless grammatical subjects. Russell puts it thus: "Whenever the grammatical subject of a proposition can be supposed not to exist without rendering the proposition meaning-

19

less, it is plain that the grammatical subject is not a proper name, i.e., not a name directly representing some object."[3] Since definite descriptions stand in no semantical relation to their *descripta,* they are incomplete symbols requiring "definition in use." The argument shows only that *some* definite descriptions are incomplete symbols, the improper ones. Russell, however, holds that *all* definite descriptions are incomplete symbols, and there is also an argument to show this.

> By an extension of the above argument, it can easily be shown that $(\imath x)$ (φx) is *always* an incomplete symbol. Take, for example, the following proposition: 'Scott is the author of *Waverley*'. (Here 'the author of *Waverley*' is $(\imath x)$ $(x$ wrote *Waverley*$)$.) This proposition expresses an identity; thus if 'the author of *Waverley*' could be taken as a proper name, and supposed to stand for some object c, the proposition would be 'Scott is c'. But if c is any one except Scott, this proposition is false; while if c is Scott, the proposition is 'Scott is Scott', which is trivial, and plainly different from 'Scott is the author of *Waverley*'. Generalizing, we see that the proposition $a = (\imath x)$ (φx) is one which may be true or may be false, but is never merely trivial, like $a = a$; whereas, if $(\imath x)$ (φx) were a proper name, $a = (\imath x)$ (φx) would necessarily be either false or the same as the trivial proposition $a = a$.[4]

Conclusion: $(\imath x)$ (φx), proper or improper, is never a (logically) proper name. Hence $(\imath x)$ (φx) is always an incomplete symbol; this is the only alternative.

It is sometimes maintained that Russell's argument rests upon a confusion of meaning and denotation. If we suppose that 'the author of *Waverley*' stands for some object c, then according to Russell, 'Scott is the author of *Waverley*' just means 'Scott is c'. The assumption here is that since 'c' names c, then assuming that 'the author of *Waverley*' names c, it follows that 'c' means the same as 'the author of *Waverley*'. But this follows, it is maintained, only if meaning is naming, only if names for the same thing mean the same thing.

This objection is not well taken. Russell's argument that definite descriptions are incomplete symbols is a *reductio ad absurdum* of the assumption that they are (logically) proper names, that is, symbols whose meanings are their denotations. Now if 'the author of *Waverley*' is a proper name, it stands for some object *c* which is its meaning, that is, 'the author of *Waverley*' means the same as '*c*' which is, by assumption, a name whose meaning is *c*. Hence if 'the author of *Waverley*' is a name for *c*, 'Scott is the author of *Waverley*' does mean 'Scott is *c*'. At times Russell puts his case in such a way as to invite the objection that he is just confusing meaning and denotation—a rather gross distinction, after all. Here is a passage of this kind: "For 'the author of *Waverley*' cannot mean the same as 'Scott' or 'Scott is the author of *Waverley*' would mean the same as 'Scott is Scott' which it plainly does not; nor can 'the author of *Waverley*' mean anything other than 'Scott' or 'Scott is the author of *Waverley*' would be false. Hence 'the author of *Waverley*' means nothing."[5] Less misleadingly stated, the conclusion of Russell's argument is that 'the author of *Waverley*' does not stand for an object as does a name.

In the opening passages of Frege's "On Sense and Reference" there is the same argument and in part the same conclusion. "The discovery that the rising sun is not new every morning, but always the same, was one of the most fertile astronomical discoveries. Even today the identification of a small planet or comet is not always a matter of course. Now if we were to regard equality as a relation between that which the names '*a*' and '*b*' designate, it would seem that $a=b$ could not differ from $a=a$ (i.e., provided $a=b$ is true). A relation would thereby be expressed of a thing to itself, and indeed one in which each thing stands to itself but to no other thing."[6] Statements of identity sometimes express important scientific information. But if the whole meaning of the terms '*a*' and '*b*' is their denotation, then $a=b$ can only convey the same information as $a=a$ (provided that $a=b$ is true). Frege concluded that besides the denotation of a term we must recognize its *sense,* which is the mode of presentation of that which is designated.

Russell and Frege agree that these considerations about identity-statements show that the (whole) meaning of a definite description cannot be its denotation. Russell concludes that definite descriptions are not in the business of standing for objects at all; there is no such relation as denoting. It is a logical mirage. Frege concludes that besides the denotation of a term, we must recognize its sense. Denotation is, for him, genuinely a relation between names and their denotations. Denoting is not the whole, but only one part of what names are in the business of doing. Russell's argument does assume that proper names are complete symbols. The meaning of a proper name is its denotation. This is often taken to be a mistake. Wittgenstein said that we must not confuse the meaning of a name with the bearer of the name, and he must have had Russell as well as his former self in mind. Russell never presents an argument to show that the meaning of a proper name (a logically proper name) is its denotation. Rather he explains that what he means by a logically proper name is one whose meaning is its denotation. "We have, then, two things to compare: (1) a *name*, which is a simple symbol, directly designating an individual which is its meaning, and having this meaning in its own right, independently of the meanings of all other words; (2) a *description*."[7]

There is still the question of whether ordinary language contains logically proper names. Russell thought that what are ordinarily called "proper names" are ordinarily not logically proper names but disguised or truncated descriptions. He also thought that the demonstratives 'this' and 'that' came close to being logically proper names, expressions whose meanings are just their changing denotations. But whether or not there actually are any logically proper names in ordinary language is a matter of indifference to the soundness of Russell's argument that definite descriptions are incomplete symbols, not proper names.

Russell appeals to the informativeness of some true identity-statements to support his conclusion that definite descriptions are not proper names. His argument is sound. Frege, not using the notion of a logically proper name (a term whose meaning is its reference), appeals to the informativeness of these true identity-statements to support his conclusion that with singular terms we must distinguish sense and reference. This argument is also sound. The different conclusions arise from the fact that each employs concepts that the other does not. Russell tried to account for the "cognitive value" of true identities using his distinction between logically proper names and incomplete symbols. Frege instead employed the sense/reference distinction. Neither pair of distinctions is forced upon us as the only possible or "correct" one. What we have are alternative theories applied to the same facts. It is surely time that philosophers stop repeating that Russell's argument confuses meaning (or sense) with reference. It makes as little sense to complain that Frege has failed to distinguish ordinary proper names from logically proper names.

II

Russell held not only that the meaning of a logically proper name is its denotation, he held that there could be no such thing as an empty logically proper name, one without a denotation. Of the purported proper name 'Romulus', he says, "If it were really a name, the question of existence could not arise, because a name has got to name something or it is not a name, and if there is no such person as Romulus there cannot be a name for that person who is not there, so that this single word 'Romulus' is really a sort of truncated or telescoped description, and if you think of it as a name you will get into logical errors."[8] Russell does not say what logical errors are involved in supposing that there are empty proper names. Of course, he means by a "logically proper name" one whose meaning is its denotation, but from this it does not follow that proper names, ordinarily so-called, are none of them without a denotation. Such names would be without a meaning in Russell's sense. But why must all names have a meaning in this sense? Russell's views on this subject can be seen to be imposed upon him by his logic.

Consider Russell's theorem 10.1. $\vdash : (x)\varphi x . \supset .\varphi y$. Small Latin letters in *Principia* represent free variables, but in their occurrence in theorems of the system, they are to be understood as unspecified constants, proper names. This principle 10.1, of "specification" says that if everything has φ so does y, that is, this principle just says (in the formal mode) that every individual constant denotes something. Again, consider "existential generalization," $\vdash : \varphi y . \supset . (\exists x) \varphi x$. This says that if y has φ, something has φ, and this is just another way of saying (in the formal mode of speech) that every individual constant (proper name) denotes something.

The validity of these classical laws of logic presupposes that all names have denotation. Following Jaakko Hintikka, we may say that classical predicate logic rests upon "existential presuppositions."[9] These existential presuppositions can be eliminated by elevating them to the status of explicit additional premisses. We thus arrive at a logic "free" from existential presuppositions. What is required for free logic is a predicate of existence. In free logic, the inference by specification is modified to allow the conclusion $F(a)$ not from $(x)F(x)$ alone, but only together with the additional premiss 'a exists'. Similarly the inference to $(\exists x)F(x)$ by existential generalization from $F(a)$ requires, in free logic, the same additional premiss assuring the existence of a.

Quine tells us that "to be is to be a value of a bound variable." Since in classical predicate logic every constant denotes an object in the range of the quantifiers, $(\exists x) (x=a)$ is a valid sentence in that logic, for it says that a is a value of a bound variable, that is, that a exists.[10] "To be is to be a value of a bound variable," is just what this theorem says. It is no more controversial than the platitude that to eat is to eat something.[11] Because $(\exists x) (x=a)$ is a valid sentence, it cannot be a required premiss in an argument formulated in classical logic. The distinguishing characteristic of free logic is its admission of empty singular terms. If quantifiers continue to range over all that exists in free logic, then when 'b' is an empty name $(\exists x) (x=b)$ will be false. Being not valid, $(\exists x) (x=b)$ does express the required premiss of existence in a logic free of existential presuppositions.[12] There remain alternative ways of accommodating vacuous names. In some versions of free logic they too denote, only their denotations are, in Meinongian fashion, unreal things in an outer domain, that is, outside the range of the quantifiers. In other treatments, they have no denotation at all.

Granted that Russell's doctrine that there cannot be vacuous names is embedded in the existential presuppositions of his logic (and indeed in all versions of classical predicate logic), there is still the question with respect to this matter of vacuity, how similar Russell's logically proper names are to what are ordinarily called proper names in natural languages. Are there vacuous names in ordinary language? Just what is a vacuous name? Is 'Santa Claus' a vacuous name, or is it rather the name of a make-believe character? If we take the second alternative, it is hard to see how we could come up with examples of vacuous names in actual use. But, of course, we do use names of non-existent or unreal things, for example, 'Santa Claus', and if that is what is meant by a "vacuous" name, there are plenty of them in ordinary language.

III

The distinguishing characteristic of free logic is the presence of empty names. For a Russellian, free logic will seem insufficiently motivated. Why not translate the purported empty names into improper Russellian descriptions? Quine has shown us how to replace all singular terms by definite descriptions. So the translations present no difficulty. Will the resulting logic of empty names be correct? Are there significant differences between free logic and Russell's theory of definite descriptions as regards their respective accounts of the logic of empty names? If there are, which is better?

Consider the similarities. Definite descriptions for Russell, like proper names in free logic, are not always substitutable for free variables. Improper descriptions are not substitutable in the one theory, just as empty names are not in the other. In free logic, specification requires a premiss guaranteeing nonemptiness of the name to which specification is made. In Russell's theory of descriptions, specification requires an additional premiss of existence, E!($\imath x$) (φx), to be added to the premiss (x) ($\psi(x)$). Without this we may not infer $\psi(\imath x)$ (φx). For existential generalization, the situation is complicated by considerations of scope. $\psi(\imath x)$ (φx).$\supset$.($\exists x$)ψx is a theorem in *Principia*. This looks like existential generalization in the theory of descriptions. It seems that here we do have a contrast, since the added existence premiss is missing. This, however, ignores the scope distinctions required by Russell's theory, for $\sim$[($\imath x$) (φx)]:$\psi(\imath x)$ (φx): $\supset$.($\exists x$) $\sim \psi x$ also looks like existential generalization in the theory of descriptions and it is not a theorem without addition of the existence premiss thus, ($\sim$[($\imath x$)(φx)]:$\psi(\imath x)$ (φx)) &E! ($\imath x$) (φx):$\supset$.($\exists x$) $\sim \psi x$. This is exactly analogous to existential generalization in free logic, with definite descriptions replacing proper names. So, improper descriptions in *Principia* are the surrogates for the empty names of free logic. The predicate of existence is present in the form E! ($\imath x$) (φx). This, like its analogue ($\exists x$) ($x=a$) in free logic, is sometimes false.

Are there reasons to prefer one account over the other? Certainly the friends of free logic will object to Russell's theorem $\psi(\imath x)$ (φx).$\supset$.E!($\imath x$) (φx). When improper Russellian descriptions act as surrogates for empty names, this theorem requires the falsity of every proposition containing empty names (in primary occurrence). This is objectionable to the friends of free logic, for a principal motive for their undertaking is to represent some such propositions as truths. Anyone content to regard 'Santa Claus lives at the North Pole' as false will be able to live with Russell's version of this treating 'Santa Claus' as a disguised description having primary occurrence. Anyone sympathetic to free logic will at least maintain that Santa Claus= Santa Claus, whether or not Santa Claus exists. Russell's version of this makes it false because it requires one of the occurrences of the description replacing 'Santa Claus' to have primary occurrence (the leftmost, unless otherwise indicated by a scope operator).

There are arguments supporting the Russellian view. If Santa Claus does not exist, how can it be true that he lives at the North Pole? Living at the North Pole is not something that a nonbeing is up to. And self-identity, though a property of everything, is hardly something that a nonbeing can have. Still, appeals to intuition in this matter yield conflicting results. We feel that a person who says 'Santa Claus lives at the South Pole' has gone wrong in some radical way in which the person who says that 'Santa Claus lives at the North Pole' has not. So a distinction seems overlooked in any theory which uniformly marks them both false. And 'Santa Claus=Santa Claus' seems the least we must admit if we are to use the name 'Santa Claus' at all. But how can a nonbeing be anything?

The cause of these vacillations is easy to locate. If it is clear that 'Santa Claus lives at the North Pole' is being said in the course of telling a Christmas story, it would not occur to us to mark the statement as false. If, on the other hand, these words were said in serious discourse on the inhabitants of the polar regions, we would mark them as mistaken. If queried as to the truth-value of the sentence without reference to a context of utterance, we vacillate between 'true' and 'false' while relativizing the question to one context of utterance after the other. But neither Russell's logic, nor any other yet devised, can reflect the change of truth-value which accompanies the shift from story telling to "serious" discourse. The bearers of truth-values in classical semantics are sentences (or propositions), not utterances in a context. Or, these sentences (or propositions) can just be thought of as utterances produced in the context of "serious" scientific discourse. Then one can see why Frege thought it a defect of our language that it even allowed the possibility of empty names. This is not a defect from the point of view of one who wishes to write a novel!

IV

The distinguishing characteristics of Russell's theory of definite descriptions are all consequential upon his treatment of the *waste cases*, the improper descriptions. These distinguishing characteristics are the doctrines of descriptions as incomplete symbols, their contextural definition "in use," and their scope ambiguity. An example will serve to show this. Consider the proposition $\sim\psi(\imath x)(\varphi x)$. For Russell's purposes it was important that this proposition be subject to two interpretations, according to whether the scope of the description is taken as wide or narrow. For this proposition to be the contradictory of $\psi(\imath x)(\varphi x)$, the scope of the description must be taken to be as small as possible. On this interpretation $\sim\psi(\imath x)(\varphi x)$ abbreviates $\sim[(\exists c)((x)((\varphi x)\equiv(x=c))\&(\psi c))]$. This is true whenever $(\imath x)(\varphi x)$ is improper. The other interpretation of $\sim\psi(\imath x)(\varphi x)$ accords the description a wide scope. Thus understood, $\sim\psi(\imath x)(\varphi x)$ abbreviates $(\exists c)[(x)(\varphi x.\equiv.x=c)\&\sim\psi c]$. This is false whenever $(\imath x)(\varphi x)$ is improper. The contradictory of $\psi(\imath x)(\varphi x)$ is thus $\sim\psi(\imath x)(\varphi x)$ with the description given narrow scope. The ambiguity in the negative form $\sim\psi(\imath x)(\varphi x)$ is induced by the impropriety of the description. For Russell, a principal motive for developing his theory was to provide for nondenoting descriptions. With these he would solve the problem of the logical analysis of negative existentials. So, of course, he did not regard the ambiguities induced by improper descriptions as a mark against his analysis.

The case of negation can be generalized, and Russell emphasized this in the concluding portions of his formal treatment of descriptions in *14 of *Principia*. Introducing this section, he says, "The purpose of the following propositions is to show that, when E! $(\imath x)(\varphi x)$, the scope of $(\imath x)(\varphi x)$ does not matter to the truth-value of any proposition in which $(\imath x)(\varphi x)$ occurs. . . . The proposition can be proved generally when $(\imath x)(\varphi x)$ occurs in the form $\chi(\imath x)(\varphi x)$ and $\chi(\imath x)(\varphi x)$ occurs in what we may call a 'truth-function', i.e., a function whose truth or falsehood depends only upon the truth or falsehood of its argument or arguments. This covers all the cases with which we are ever concerned. That is to say, if $\chi(\imath x)(\varphi x)$ occurs in any of the ways which can be generated by the processes of *1—*11, then provided E! $(\imath x)(\varphi x)$, the truth-value of $f[(\imath x)(\varphi x)].\chi(\imath x)(\varphi x)$ is the same as that of $[(\imath x)(\varphi x)].f\{\chi(\imath x)(\varphi x)\}$." What Russell is saying is that, as long as the only modes of statement composition which are allowed are truth-functional, the only way in which scope ambiguities can arise is by being induced through nondenoting (improper) descriptions. If descriptions are so treated that impropriety is excluded, as with Frege, the need for a device, such as Russell's scope operator, for the disambiguation of propositions containing descriptions will not exist. But note that Russell says, "This covers all the cases with which we are ever concerned." This must be understood to mean "all the cases with which we are ever concerned in extensional (truth-functional) logic." When non-truth-functional forms of composition occur, as with logical necessity and the propositional attitudes, *then even proper descriptions induce scope ambiguities*. This may be taken to be a characteristic logical mark of such propositions. The full importance of the observation italicized in the next to the last sentence was not appreciated for many years after the publication of *Principia*. From this present perspective, we can be happy that Russell developed the theory of scope ambiguities induced by descriptions. But Russell also showed that he was aware of a way of avoiding them in truth-functional logic. In Frege's treatment of descriptions for extensional logic there are no improper descriptions; hence, no scope ambiguity. In nonextensional contexts Frege also admitted an ambiguity concerning singular terms, not of scope but of reference. What is ordinarily the sense of a singular term is its reference in nonextensional contexts. So in these cases also Frege avoided the need for a theory of scope ambiguities induced by descriptions. It was a matter of methodological importance for Frege that they be avoided, for Frege wished to treat descriptions uniformly with proper names from a logical point of view.

It is sometimes said that the logical difference between proper names and definite descriptions is that the latter induce scope ambiguity and the former do not. If we add to this that, on the intended interpretation of *Principia*, proper names (logically proper names) can freely replace free variables and be replaced by free variables in theorems, we attain a full account of the logical differences between (logically) proper names and definite descriptions in Russell's treatment of the subject. In Frege's treatment all these differences disappear. Once he eliminates improper descriptions by providing an arbitrary object for them to denote (or by assigning $(\imath x)\,(\varphi x)$ the value $\hat{x}(\varphi x)$ in case φx is not uniquely satisfied, as in *Grundgesetze*) all of the logical differences between proper names and descriptions are removed. Thus Frege is in a position to provide a uniform semantics for both. From his point of view both are *eigennamen*. But Frege did not exclude vacuous singular terms from his *Begriffsschrift* primarily in order to attain a smooth running general theory.

Frege regarded it as an imperfection of ordinary language that it allowed the occurrence of singular terms lacking denotation. He is careful to exclude this possibility, together with other defects of ordinary language such as ambiguity, from his *Begriffsschrift*. Of nondenoting singular terms he says,

> This arises from an imperfection of language, from which even the symbolic language of mathematical analysis is not altogether free; even there combinations of symbols can occur that seem to stand for something but have (at least so far) no reference, e.g., divergent infinite series. This can be avoided, e.g., by means of the special stipulation that divergent infinite series shall stand for the number 0. A logically perfect language (*Begriffsschrift*) should satisfy the conditions, that every expression grammatically well constructed as a proper name out of signs already introduced shall in fact designate an object, and that no new sign shall be introduced as a proper name without being secured a reference.[13]

In *Grundgesetze*, Frege adhered to these principles in the introduction of his "*Ersatz* for the definite article." Using Russell's notation, and avoiding special features of this account not relevant here, a Fregean theory of descriptions along the lines of *Grundgesetze* may be presented as follows: $(\imath x)\,(\varphi x)$ is a singular term in primitive notation. It is constructed by applying the variable binding description operator $\imath$ to the open sentence φx. In case exactly one element of the domain of discourse satisfies φx, '$(\imath x)\,(\varphi x)$' denotes that element. Otherwise '$(\imath x)\,(\varphi x)$' denotes $\hat{x}(\varphi x)$, the class of things which satisfies φx. An alternative treatment of the latter case suggested in the passage cited above from

"On Sense and Reference" provides a unique denotation selected once and for all for the improper case, for example 0.

Frege's treatment of the improper case yields a theory of descriptions which deprives them of all of the special logical characteristics which in the *Principia* treatment serve to distinguish them from logically proper names. For Frege, definite descriptions, like Russell's logically proper names, are complete symbols which denote. They are not introduced by contextual definition, but belong in the primitive notation. Like proper names they do not suffer from scope ambiguity. Further, descriptions in Frege's treatment are freely substitutable for proper names in inferences by specification and existential generalization. These would seem to be considerable advantages for the Fregean approach and if there are no corresponding disadvantages, it would seem reasonable to conclude that before Russell presented his theory of descriptions in "On Denoting" in 1905, Frege had already discovered a superior treatment of the subject.

What strikes an odd note in Frege's theory is its arbitrary handling of the improper cases as "don't cares." The motivation is clear. What is gained is formal simplicity and a smooth running general treatment of singular terms. Elegance is bought at the price of naturalness. For Frege, it is a matter of indifference what truth-value is assigned to propositions containing improper descriptions in primary occurrence. Russell makes all such propositions false and surely this is no less arbitrary. In "serious" fact-stating discourse conducted in ordinary language, we do not make statements containing definite descriptions in primary occurrence which we know to be vacuous, so ordinary language provides no guide for a correct distribution of truth-values for these propositions (unless it provides the intuition that such propositions simply lack truth-values). In any case, there is no foundation in linguistic intuition for preferring Russell's theory over Frege's on this count.

Let a^* designate the bearer of all descriptions $(\imath x)(\varphi x)$ for which φx is not uniquely satisfied. The following formula is valid for a theory of descriptions using a^* in this way: $\{\psi(\imath x)(\varphi x)\} \equiv \{(\exists c)[(x)((\varphi x) \equiv (x=c))\&\psi c]V[\sim(\exists c)(x)((\varphi x) \equiv (x=c))$

31

&$\psi a*$]}. This presents an unintuitive disjunction in the truth-conditions for propositions containing descriptions. If ψ ($\imath x$) (φx) is true, it may be because the unique satisfier of φx satisfies ψx as well, or it may be because φx is not uniquely satisfied and $a*$ satisfies ψx. It comes as a shock to our linguistic intuitions that besides the expected first way in which $\psi(\imath x)$ (φx) might express a truth, there is this *radical* second way; the proposition might be, we may say, "radically true." But on this score Russell is no better off, because for him there is a corresponding disjunction in the falsity-conditions for $\psi(\imath x)$ (φx) which, if false, is so either because the unique satisfier of φx fails to satisfy ψx or because there is no unique satisfier of φx. So while Frege, against Russell, allows for the radical truth of ψ ($\imath x$) (φx) as well as its simple truth, Russell allows only for the radical falsehood of our proposition. Frege does as well. For Frege $\psi(\imath x)$ (φx) could be false either because the unique satisfier of φx fails to satisfy ψx or because there is no unique satisfier of φx and $a*$ fails to satisfy ψx.[14]

Both radical truth and radical falsehood run counter to our linguistic intuitions. Frege recognized this when he said, "If anything is asserted there is always an obvious presupposition that the simple or compound proper names used have reference. If one therefore asserts 'Kepler died in misery', there is a presupposition that the name 'Kepler' designates something; but it does not follow that the sense of the sentence 'Kepler died in misery' contains the thought that the name 'Kepler' designates something."[15] Now if we replace 'Kepler' in this example by a definite description this remark becomes applicable to Russell's theory of descriptions because in the theorem $\psi(\imath x)$ (φx). $\supset$ .E!($\imath x$) (φx) Russell provides that part of the thought expressed by any proposition containing a description, in primary occurrence, is the thought that the description designates something. It is because this thought may be false that we get Russell's radical falsehood. It is not enough to provide that every singular term designate something in order to settle our problem. Frege, as we have seen, does that in *Grundgesetze*, with the result that we get radical truths as well as radical falsehoods. In order to eliminate *both* these possibilities we need not only provide that '$(\imath x)(\varphi x)$' always has a denotation, we need to provide that it denotes the right thing, $(\imath x)(\varphi x)$. This is what Meinong does with his pure object. For Meinong, '$(\imath x)(\varphi x)$' always denotes $(\imath x)(\varphi x)$, even though $(\imath x)(\varphi x)$ may not exist. The realm of objects is far wider than all that exists. To think otherwise is to fall victim to that *prejudice in favor of the actual* which Meinong deplored.[16] Some objects exist and some do not; some subsist and some do not. "Those who like paradoxical modes of expression could very well say: 'There are objects of which it is true that there are no such objects'."[17] (*"Es gibt Gegenstände, von denen gilt, dass es dergleichen Gegenstände nicht gibt."*) $(\imath x)(\varphi x)$ denotes the pure object in all its indifference to being and nonbeing. The pure object is beyond being and not being, *jenseits von Sein und Nichtsein*. Meinong combines this doctrine of the *Aussersein* of the pure object with the principle of the independence of *Sosein* from *Sein;* an object's posession of properties is independent of the being of the object in any sense.[18] This is the denial of Russell's fundamental theorem, $\psi(\imath x)(\varphi x) . \supset .E!(\imath x)(\varphi x)$. Meinong uses the example of the gold mountain which both does not exist and is made of gold.[19] This commits Meinong to the universal validity of the formula $\varphi(\imath x)(\varphi x)$, against Russell. This formula expresses a special case of the independence of *Sosein* from *Sein* and it is a consequence of Meinong's first principle that '$(\imath x)(\varphi x)$' always denotes the "right" object. So the two basic principles of Meinong's theory of denoting are not logically independent.

With Meinong we avoid both radical truth and radical falsehood, but apparently only at the price of contradiction. Russell says in "On Denoting," referring to "pure objects," "Such objects are apt to infringe the law of contradiction. It is contended, that the present king of France exists and does not exist; that the round square is round and also not round, etc. But this is intolerable; and if any theory can be found to avoid this result, it is surely to be preferred."[20]

As I see him, Meinong is far from being the prime example of the extravagant metaphysician he is usually taken to be. Seen against the background of the alternative theories of Russell and Frege, Meinong appears as the advocate of a middle way which avoids both radical truth and radical falsehood. In this his view accords with our linguistic intuitions. Meinong's fundamental thought is that phrases of the form '$(\imath x)(\varphi x)$' always denote something, and, here he agrees with the spirit of Frege's *Begriffsschrift*. But Meinong insists, against Frege, that what phrases of this form denote is always $(\imath x)(\varphi x)$, and this is certainly closer to our intuitions than Frege's account according to which '$(\imath x)(\varphi x)$', if improper, denotes anything you like, provided the entity is fixed once and for all. The insistance that '$(\imath x)(\varphi x)$' denote the right thing leads immediately to a special case of the independence of *Sosein* from *Sein*, for it entails that $\varphi(\imath x)(\varphi x)$ is always true for any choice of φ; and the immediate consequence of this is the apparent violation of the law of contradiction noted by Russell. By the above principle 'the round square', that is, $(\imath x)(Rx.Sx)$, is *both* round and square, $R(\imath x)(Rx.Sx)\&$ $S(\imath x)(Rx.Sx)$. Assuming that what is square is not round we have the contradiction $R(\imath x)(Rx.Sx)\&\sim R(\imath x)(Rx.Sx)$.

One might think it a plausible move at this point to adopt a restricted Meinongian position according to which the theory applies only to descriptions $(\imath x)(\varphi x)$ where φx is logically consistent, thus excluding cases such as $(\imath x)(Rx.Sx)$, because of the inconsistency of $Rx.Sx$. This accords with the intuition which motivated Meinong but apparently leads to a similar contradiction in another way.[21] The problem now concerns the *compossibility* of several descriptions, each of which is self-consistent, each denoting the right object. Consider for example the descriptions 'the fat mother of Richard Nixon' and 'the thin mother of Richard Nixon'. According to our restricted Meinongian theory there must be a unique person who is both fat and thin to be denotation of both of these consistent descriptions, at least on the assumption that Richard Nixon has only one mother. So, in the end, this narrow range version is no less objectionable than the full-dress Meinongian theory.

I have interpreted Russell's remark that Meinong's objects are "apt to infringe the law of contradiction" as a claim that

Meinong's theory is actually inconsistent, and this view is widely held. I have attempted to derive this contradiction concerning the round square. It has been shown that Meinong's principles lead to the conclusion that it is both round and square. Something like this derivation must have been in Russell's mind when he made the remark about Meinong's objects violating the law of contradiction. But notice that the argument for inconsistency is based on a premiss which Meinong would certainly reject, the premiss that what is square is not round. Of course no actual square is round, but the round square is a nonexistent square and Meinong would surely object that it is both round and square. Thus the premiss used to derive the contradiction $R(\imath x) (Rx.Sx)$ $\&\sim R(\imath x) (Rx.Sx)$ is not true of the round square. There is no contradiction, that is, no proposition of the form $p\&\sim p$ which has been derived from Meinong's principles. Further, Meinong would maintain that the assertion that the round square is both round and square is not paradoxical, given that it not only is nonexistent but an impossible object. Meinong could object similarly to the attempted derivation of a contradiction from the restricted theory according to which terms that denote objects cannot be formed from inconsistent sentences such as 'Round (x) & Square (x)'. According to this view the thin mother of Nixon is an object and so is the fat mother of Nixon. But why can Nixon not have more than one mother, so long as not more than one of them exists? The view that each person has only one mother is but another example of our "prejudice in favor of the actual."

Russell objected further to these views that if the round square is both round and square, the existent round square must be round, square, and existent. He claimed thus, that it followed from Meinong's principles that the round square *exists*! But Meinong could surely have objected to this that all that Russell had done was to produce an argument from Meinong's own principles to show that *existence* is not genuinely a predicate.[22]

Frege and Russell provide theories of reference for formal languages which conflict, at points, with our intuitions about reference in natural languages. Meinong comes nearest to capturing these intuitions and his theory does not seem to lead to contradiction as it is widely supposed to do. What disturbs us about his ontological population explosion, I believe, is that these objects have no clear identity-conditions. Is the present king of France identical with or different from the present king of China? There seem to be no principles which can be used to provide an answer to such questions. One answer is as reasonable as the other and this makes the very notion of an *object* seem misapplied here.

Neither Russell, Frege, nor Meinong provides a completely adequate account of vacuous singular terms in natural languages. Russell aimed to provide such an account in his formal theory but this is not so for Frege. In his *Begriffsschrift* Frege saw not a theory of natural language but an improved language which avoided the defects of natural languages. One such defect, for him, is that in natural languages there are vacuous singular terms. For this reason it is wrong to criticize Frege's formal theory on grounds of unnaturalness. As far as natural languages are concerned, Frege held that vacuous singular terms induce truth-value gaps (or an oblique context, in the case of 'exists'). This is brought out in the quotation about 'Kepler' cited above. It may be instructive to look briefly at Frege's formal language from his point of view, that is, as an alternative to natural language rather than as a theory of the latter. Suppose we are told, 'The present king of France is bald'. A Russellian decides that this proposition is false on discovering that France is not a monarchy, hence the radical falsity. A Fregean making the same discovery still has to consider the designated entity a^* before assigning our proposition a truth-value. Suppose a^* *is* bald, then for him, our proposition is true. Does this not make his language less efficient than the Russellian's? I think not, for if our Fregean is interested in the proposition 'The present king of France is bald', he will lose all interest in its truth-value on discovering that France is not a monarchy. He knows that the semantical rules of his language will assign a truth-value to it according to the choice of a^*, but the mere fact that the proposition is true has no consequences of interest for him. He has first to determine what fact about the world makes it true. So this is a perfectly good language and leads to no misunderstanding between the Fregean and the Russellian. For example, if the Russellian decides that our proposition is false and the Fregean that it is true, they can still each see that they both agree entirely as to the facts. What facts? That France is not a monarchy and that a^* is bald! Thus our criticism of Frege's theory as a theory of natural language leaves unchallenged his claim that his language is an improved one.

V

Russell held that definite descriptions are incomplete symbols because he did not see any other way of making significant denials of singular existence possible. We cannot first assume that an object exists and then go on to deny this. Meinong had posed the problem earlier and went on to provide an answer which Russell could not accept. A main motivation behind Russell's theory of descriptions is to answer Meinong's problem while avoiding his solution. When Russell dealt with the matter earlier in the *Principles of Mathematics*, he had arrived, as we have seen, at a position close to that of Meinong. By 1905 this view had come to seem to be a violation of the robust sense of reality necessary in dealing with abstract subjects. Frege, we have seen, provides a denotation for all descriptions. How then does he deal with these troublesome negative existential propositions? Frege would certainly have objected to Russell's notation $E!(\imath x)(\varphi x)$, because it seems to treat existence as a property of objects. For Frege quantifiers are second-level concepts within which first-level concepts fall. For Frege, $(\exists x)\varphi x$ names a second-level concept. That it is a concept-name is indicated by the occurrence of the Greek letter which *indefinitely indicates* first-level concepts. A first-level concept falls within this second-level concept if and only if it is instantiated. $(\exists x)Fx$ says that the concept F is instantiated. Existence is a property of concepts, not a property of objects. Thus, for Frege, $\sim E!(\imath x)(\varphi x)$ is a bad piece of notation because it predicates nonexistence of the object $(\imath x)(\varphi x)$. Properly expressed, what we are denying is that a certain first-level concept

37

has instances. That concept is $(x)(\varphi x. \equiv .x=c)$. We assert its noninstantiation in the proposition $\sim(\exists c)(x)(\varphi x. \equiv .x=c)$, and this may very well be true in spite of the fact that $(\imath x)(\varphi x)$ always has a denotation. Remember that, for Frege, the denotation of $(\imath x)(\varphi x)$ need not satisfy φx at all.

Of course, for Russell too, existence is not really a property of objects, it only appears to be because of the predicative position of E! in the abbreviated notation of *Principia*. In primitive notation E! disappears, leaving only the quantifier to express existence. Russell even adopts Frege's mode of description in saying that existence is a property of propositional functions.[23]

This account of Frege's treatment of negative existentials is perhaps overly Russellian. He does not explicitly deal with the matter since he thought it a defect of natural languages that they allowed vacuous singular terms. It is a defect because vacuous terms induce truth-value gaps in any (declarative) sentence containing them. From this observation and some others we can construct the Fregean account of negative existentials in natural languages which was presented in chapter 1. According to this account, 'exists' induces an oblique (*ungerade*) context and in the proposition 'Pegasus does not exist', 'Pegasus' denotes what is ordinarily its sense. This is, I think, a rather satisfactory result since it exploits the intuition that existence-contexts are indeed special, and that what prevents our proposition from being meaningless is the fact that the denotationless name is not devoid of sense.

VI

In section I, Russell's argument that definite descriptions are incomplete symbols was defended against the charge that it rests on a confusion of meaning and reference. But are definite descriptions incomplete symbols? Is this view in agreement with our linguistic intuitions concerning ordinary language? What it means is that descriptions in ordinary language, unlike proper names, are simply not in the business of denoting (referring, standing for, naming) at all. What makes the view plausible is the waste case of vacuous descriptions. 'The present king of France' is not in the business of standing for an object. But the intuition is surely just as clear that 'the present queen of England' does stand for an object, Elizabeth II. Russell complements his theory of definite descriptions with a theory of "indefinite descriptions," phrases of the form 'all men', 'no men', 'some men'.²⁴ Such phrases really are all incomplete symbols, syncategorematic expressions which contribute to the meanings of the propositions containing them, but they do not stand for objects.

The argument for these conclusions is quite conclusive. If I meet a man, there must be some definite man whom I meet, but my assertion 'I met a man' is not of the subject/predicate form attributing the property of being met by me to some "ambiguous object," a man. The result of replacing the indefinite description 'a man' in the assertion 'I met a man' by a proper name, say 'Socrates', is an assertion of the subject/predicate form, but the result of the replacement is a complete change in the logical form of the original. 'A man' in 'I met a man', simply does not have the role of a singular term. We cannot conclude 'A man=a man' from the premiss $(x)(x=x)$ for this "conclusion" is just nonsense. 'A man' cannot flank the identity sign. If 'All men' were a singular term in 'All men are mortal' there would be no logical difference between '∼All men are mortal' and 'All men are not mortal', any more than there is a logical difference between 'Socrates is not mortal' and '∼Socrates is mortal'. Singular terms are indifferent to the distinction between *inner* and *outer* negation. Again from 'All men are mortal' it does not follow that $(\exists x)$ (x is mortal); we cannot quantify out an indefinite description as we can a singular term. So far Russell's argument that indefinite descriptions are incomplete symbols is quite parallel to his argument that definite descriptions are not proper names.

Russell went on to introduce definite descriptions by contextual definition. Why did he not do the same for indefinite descriptions, since the arguments for doing this are exactly the same as those which he used in the case of definite descriptions?²⁵ Consider the proposition 'All swans are white'. We could introduce the indefinite description $(\iota x)(Sx)$ to represent 'All swans' and represent 'All swans are white' as a subject/predicate proposition, $W(\iota x)(Sx)$. This latter could be defined contextually using a scope operator for indefinite descriptions:

$$[(\iota x)(Sx)]W(\iota x)(Sx) . = . (x)(Sx \supset Wx) \text{ Df.}$$

The treatment of the rest of the Aristotelian schedule of categorical propositions is then easily represented with the use of the indefinite description together with negation and the scope operator. 'No swans are white' is represented as

$$[(\iota x)(Sx)] \sim W(\iota x)(Sx),$$

which in accordance with our contextual definition becomes,

$$(x)(Sx \supset \sim Wx).$$

'Some swans are white' is represented as the negation of 'No swans are white',

$$\sim [(\iota x)(Sx)] \sim W(\iota x)(Sx),$$

and in primitive notation becomes

$$\sim (x)(Sx \supset \sim Wx), \text{ or } (\exists x)(Sx \& Wx).$$

'Some swans are not white' is the negation of 'All swans are white', hence

$$\sim [(\iota x)(Sx)]W(\iota x)(Sx).$$

The arguments favoring this treatment of indefinite descriptions are so closely parallel to those which Russell uses in support of his treatment of definite descriptions that if there is a serious objection to the one, it should hold for the other as well. Yet surely it will be felt that Russell was right not to introduce a special notation for indefinite descriptions into *Principia*. The notation of *Principia* was designed to yield a correct logical analysis of certain forms of propositions and what is wrong with the use of a special notation for indefinite descriptions is that it serves to obscure the true logical form of general propositions rather than to reveal their correct logical form. Although

W$(\iota x)(\varphi x)$looks grammatically like a subject/predicate proposition, its logic is quite different.

Now if we are inclined to accept the notation $(\iota x)(\varphi x)$ on the other hand as justified, it is because our intuitions tell us, contrary to Russell, that $\psi(\iota x)(\varphi x)$ really is logically of the subject/predicate form, at least as long as $(\iota x)(\varphi x)$ is proper. Indeed, this intuition is so strong that it should lead us to regard these improper descriptions as defects of natural languages like the defects of ambiguity and vagueness. We can then give way to our inclination to follow Frege in his treatment of propositions of the form $\psi(\iota x)(\varphi x)$ as genuinely of the subject/predicate form.

3

Rigid Designators

I

Saul Kripke's recent essays "Naming and Necessity" and "Identity and Necessity" attack what he regards as the view of the classical logical tradition as represented by Frege and Russell that "really a proper name, properly used, simply was a definite description abbreviated or disguised. Frege specifically said that such a description gave the sense of the name."[1] "The modern tradition," he says, "as represented by Frege and Russell disputed Mill on the issue of singular terms. . . . The present view, directly reversing Frege and Russell, *endorses* Mill's view of *singular* terms, but *disputes* his view of *general* terms."[2] Mill's view, endorsed by Kripke against Frege and Russell, is that genuine proper names have denotation but not connotation. Mill further maintained that general (or "common") names have connotation, but on this point Kripke is against Mill; he thinks that common names too have denotation but not connotation. The view of the classical logical tradition, the "Frege-Russell view" as Kripke calls it, holds, according to Kripke, that proper names are identical in sense with (synonymous with) definite descriptions. Presumably each such name is identical in sense (synonymous) with some one definite description which "by definition" determines the reference of the name.[3]

Kripke's characterization of the "Frege-Russell" view is quite mistaken. Although he says categorically, "Frege specifically said that such a description gave the sense of the name," he does not cite a text in support of this. But it is clear, in any case, that

Frege's semantical principles do not commit him to this view. Terms having the same sense must, for Frege, be everywhere intersubstitutive *salva veritate*. Frege repeatedly observed that terms identical in their customary reference generally are not intersubstitutive in belief-contexts and this proved that such terms differed in sense. Any informative identity-statement contains names which are identical in reference and different in sense. Why *should* there always be some one definite description which expresses the sense of every proper name? Just try, for example, to produce the description which expresses the sense (for you) of Kripke's favorite example, 'Richard Nixon'. In my own case there are many descriptions which I know denote him, but none which, above all the others, has the privileged role of expressing the sense I attach to that name. Why should there be one? Perhaps in the case of some few names it is the case that Kripke's condition is met, but it will not be so for most cases. I do not see how it can be concluded from this that proper names do not have sense. There will be more on this topic in chapter 4.

Throughout his papers Kripke argues against this view that a proper name has the same sense as some coreferential description. When he says again, at the end of "Naming and Necessity," that he endorses Mill's view on singular terms, he implies that having refuted the view that a name is identical in sense with some description which is coreferential with it he is entitled to conclude that names do not have sense at all but only denotation. But this does not follow. Frege held both that proper names have sense and that, in general, this sense is not the same as that of some definite description which denotes the same object as the name. From 'Phosphorus=the morning star' and 'Thales knows that Phosphorus=Phosphorus', it does not follow that 'Thales knows that Phosphorus=the morning star'. This just shows that 'Phosphorus' and 'the morning star' differ in sense. It does not show that 'Phosphorus' does not have a sense.

I think it certain that what Kripke calls the "Frege-Russell view" was not Frege's view at all. Was it Russell's view? I think it equally certain that it was not Russell's view either. For one thing, Russell held that descriptions did not have sense. He thought that the sense/reference distinction was incoherent,[4] so he could not have held that names are identical in sense with descriptions. Now, strangely enough, Kripke explicitly acknowledges this. He says, "In reporting Russell's views, we thus deviate from him in two respects. . . ; second, we regard descriptions, and their abbreviations, as having sense."[5] So Kripke knows that the view he is ascribing to Russell is not, in fact, Russell's view. After all, it goes to the heart of Russell's theory of descriptions that they are incomplete symbols lacking all meaning "in isolation" and that a correct logical analysis will reveal that they are not semantically significant units in the sentences in which they occur; not semantically significant in the sense that, as un-analyzed units, they contribute to the meaning of the whole sentence containing them.

Though Kripke acknowledges that he is misrepresenting Russell's theory, he thinks that this is justified for the following reason. "Though we won't put things the way Russell does, we could describe Russell as saying that names, as they are ordinarily called, *do* have sense. They have sense in a strong way, namely, we should be able to give a definite description such that the referent of the name, by definition, is the object satisfying the description."[6] It is of rather little interest, in and of itself, that in attacking the "Frege-Russell view," Kripke ascribes to these authors views about proper names which they did not actually hold. I have brought the matter up mainly because it will help us to see just what view Kripke himself advocates as a substitute for the so-called classical logical theory, if we are clear about what he thinks the theory he is rejecting is. So far two points have emerged: (1) Kripke holds (against Frege) that ordinary proper names do not have sense at all and (2) he holds (against Russell) that ordinary proper names cannot generally be associated with some description such that the referent of the name is "by definition" the object denoted by the description.

II

Though I have said that I am not interested in the exegesis of historical texts for its own sake, I think that it will be of help to us in seeing the philosophical issues involved in this dispute between Kripke and the classical tradition if we take some time to present the actual views of the classical authors, particularly Russell, on the relation between proper names (ordinarily so called) and definite descriptions. Russell's favorite locutions in presenting his view were that ordinary proper names are "truncated," "abbreviated," or "disguised" descriptions. In saying these things, he meant to distinguish them from logically proper names. These ways of talking are certainly in need of elucidation. What does it mean to say that an ordinary proper name is a "truncated" or "disguised" description? These characterizations are sufficiently obscure that we can see how one could (as Kripke does) take Russell to be saying just that such names are synonymous (identical in sense) with definite descriptions. But I think that something else is intended, something else which embodies a very interesting and persuasive theory, and that it is best to look at the matter in this way.

The most illuminating interpretation of what Russell means when he says that ordinary proper names are "truncated" or "disguised" descriptions is that the logical behavior of such names is just like that of definite descriptions. In *Principia Mathematica* there are symbols which represent logically proper names, and expressions for definite descriptions are introduced by contextual definition; but there are no symbols representing ordinary proper names. The reason is that Russell thought that ordinary proper names could always be represented in his formal system by descriptions without producing distortions in the logical behavior of these names. Why did he think this? To answer this question, let us first briefly compare the logical behavior of logically proper names with that of descriptions in Russell's logic. It will be assumed that when a free variable occurs in a theorem of *Principia*, it is to be interpreted as an unspecified logically proper name. (This is not the only possible interpretation of free-variable theorems. Another is the generality interpretation according to which free variables in theorems are implicitly bound by universal quantifiers at the beginning of the formula. It is in this way that free-variable theorems are to be understood in the logical writings of Frege. For my purposes I take the other interpretation.) There are, of course, remarkable differences in the logical behavior of logically proper names and definite descriptions. For example, $x=x$ is a theorem, but its analogue for descriptions $(\imath x)(\varphi x)=(\imath x)(\varphi x)$ is not. The reason is that $(\imath x)(\varphi x)$ may lack a denotation; but 'x', representing a logically proper name, cannot lack a denotation. If $(\imath x)(\varphi x)$ does lack a denotation (or is "improper" as we shall sometimes say), Russell holds that $(\imath x)(\varphi x)=(\imath x)(\varphi x)$ is false. One may well think that this is wrong because, under the stated condition, the identity simply lacks a truth-value. But if one agrees that it is false, one should be willing to say that 'Santa Claus=Santa Claus' is false for the same reason. 'Santa Claus' lacks a denotation. More generally, Russell held that $\psi(\imath x)(\varphi x)$ is false whenever $(\imath x)(\varphi x)$ is improper. Again, this may seem wrong (Russell intended to give a correct account of actual use) because under the stated condition $\psi(\imath x)(\varphi x)$ is not false but neither true nor false. But if one does agree with Russell, one should also agree that 'Santa Claus lives at the North Pole' is false too. And if one thinks that $\psi(\imath x)(\varphi x)$ lacks a truth-value when $(\imath x)(\varphi x)$ is improper, one should also hold that 'Santa Claus lives at the North Pole' lacks a truth-value.

Another free-variable theorem in Russell's logic is $(x)\varphi x .\supset. \varphi y$. It says that if everything has φ, so does y. But this is a valid sentence only so long as it is assumed that y is something, that is, that y has a denotation. Thus we cannot just conclude $\psi(\imath x)(\varphi x)$ from $(x)\psi x$, for $(\imath x)(\varphi x)$ may be improper. In order to make this instantiation valid, we need an additional premiss guaranteeing the existence of $(\imath x)(\varphi x)$, that is, E! $(\imath x)(\varphi x)$. Ordinary proper names behave like descriptions in this respect and not like logically proper names. We cannot conclude φN from $(x)\varphi x$ if 'N' is an ordinary proper name precisely because 'N' may lack a denotation.

Most important, from the present standpoint, logically proper names, unlike descriptions, induce no scope ambiguities in Russell's logic. If 'a' is a logically proper name, there is no logical difference between the interpretation of $\sim F(a)$ which takes 'a' to have the entire sentence as its scope (wide scope or "primary occurrence") and that which accords the scope of '*a*' in $\sim F(a)$ merely to $F(a)$ (narrow scope or "secondary occurrence"). That is, $\sim F(a)$ will have the same truth-value under either analysis. For this reason, Russell had no need for a "scope operator" to indicate the scope of logically proper names in his formulas. For example, in English, assuming 'Richard Nixon' to be a logically proper name, there is no logical difference between the statement 'It is not the case that Richard Nixon is a Democrat' and 'Richard Nixon is not a Democrat'. Both of these statements are of the form $\sim D(N)$. But definite descriptions do induce scope ambiguities. $\sim\varphi(\imath x)(\varphi x)$ has different truth-values, according to whether the scope of $(\imath x)(\varphi x)$ is wide or narrow, when $(\imath x)(\varphi x)$ is improper. If $(\imath x)(\varphi x)$ lacks a denotation, $\sim\varphi(\imath x)(\varphi x)$ is true if the description has secondary occurrence and false if it is accorded primary occurrence. Of course, negation is only a special case. In general, propositions containing definite descriptions have logically nonequivalent interpretations according to the scope accorded the description. Since logically proper names are guaranteed a denotation, they can never induce scope ambiguities on the ground of impropriety. Furthermore, it can be proven that impropriety is the *only ground* on which any singular term can produce scope ambiguities in *Principia*. Since ordinary proper names may lack denotations, they produce scope ambiguities under exactly the same conditions as definite descriptions.

So Russell had a very strong case for saying that ordinary proper names are "truncated descriptions," if this is understood to mean that their logical behavior is indistinguishable from that of definite descriptions. It is important to notice that, as far as purely logical considerations are concerned, the entire case for the truncated description theory of names rests upon one striking point of difference between them and logically proper names. They, like descriptions, may lack denotation. Russell's claim was that having a correct account of the logical form of propositions containing ordinary proper names, he could use this account to solve some philosophical puzzles involving them. What is the logical form of a negative singular existential proposition such

47

as 'Pegasus does not exist'? In such statements names cannot be performing their normal semantical role of denoting their bearers. Russell's answer was that such propositions have the form $\sim E!(\imath x)(\varphi x)$, where $(\imath x)(\varphi x)$ is the description abbreviated by the relevant name. This seems to provide a very adequate and intuitively appealing solution to this problem. Indeed, it seems to me that something like this account of singular negative existential assertions must be correct.

<h1 style="text-align:center">III</h1>

Nevertheless, Kripke regards these views of Russell and "the classical logical tradition" as fundamentally mistaken and, indeed, a step backward from the correct position of John Stuart Mill. His view is that Russell's theory is not just mistaken in some small ways that can be repaired, but that it is wrong from the start. His arguments against Russell fall into various classes. One class of these arguments, the only ones to be treated in this chapter, are designed to show that the logical behavior of ordinary proper names is not at all like that of definite descriptions. This may seem an extraordinary claim to the reader at this point, after we have just finished presenting Russell's rather impressive case to the contrary. What has happened is that Kripke has shifted the framework within which the logical behavior of names and descriptions is to be compared from classical extensional logic to that of quantified modal logic. For this reason, I will refer to these arguments as "the modal arguments."

There is no doubt that descriptions behave very differently in modal contexts from the way they do in extensional ones. So the question of the correctness of the disguised description theory of names has now to be reexamined within the wider framework of modal logic and we should be prepared to find it no longer acceptable. This, at any rate, is what Kripke claims to show.

The entire issue turns on the matter of scope ambiguities for descriptions in modal contexts. Quine has argued that quantification into modal contexts is unintelligible. Consider the following sentences:

(1) 9 = the number of the planets,
(2) □ (9 > 7),
(3) □ (the number of planets > 7).

Both (1) and (2) are true, and (3) is false. But (3) just follows from (1) and (2) by substitution of equals for equals. Of course, it is paradox enough that a valid logical principle appears to yield a false conclusion from true premisses; but Quine's concern is with the very intelligibility of these sentences, and in particular with quantification within the scope of a modal operator. We cannot, Quine argues, move from (2) to

$$(4)\quad (\exists x)\square(x{>}7),$$

as we should expect if '9' genuinely denotes an object in (2). Statement (4) appears to say that there is an object which is necessarily greater than 7. But what, asks Quine, could that object be? Presumably it is the number 9, in accordance with (2), but it cannot be 9, in accordance with (1), given the falsity of (3). Apparently we cannot make sense of the idea of an object having the property of being necessarily greater than 7, and for similar reasons, of any statement in which a variable is bound within the scope of a modal operator.

Soon after this argument was presented, logicians such as Arthur Smullyan and Frederick Fitch replied that it rested upon a scope fallacy. Smullyan pointed out that (3) above, involving a definite description, could either be interpreted as

$$(5)\quad [(\imath x)(\varphi x)]\square((\imath x)(\varphi x){>}7),$$

or as

$$(6)\quad \square[(\imath x)(\varphi x)]((\imath x)(\varphi x){>}7).$$

Statement (6) is an assertion of necessity *de dicto* and it is false, but it does not follow from (1) and (2) by substitution of equals for equals. Statement (3), interpreted as (5) and asserting necessity *de re*, does indeed follow from (1) and (2) but it is true, at least according to Smullyan and the friends of quantified modal logic. Thus Quine's argument that quantification into modal contexts does not make sense is claimed to rest upon a fallacy resulting from failure to take proper account of the scope ambiguities induced by definite descriptions in modal contexts.

It is not so surprising that Quine was not prepared to notice the *de dicto/de re* ambiguity induced by definite descriptions in modal contexts. We have observed above that in extensional logic descriptions produce scope ambiguity under one and only one condition, that they lack a denotation. That even proper descriptions could induce scope ambiguities in nonextensional contexts was something for which an extensional logician could be unprepared. Now we can reexamine our question. Are ordinary proper names truncated or disguised descriptions? Kripke rejects Russell's affirmative answer. His case against Russell, at least that part of it which rests upon what I am calling "the modal arguments," rests entirely on the claim that proper names, unlike descriptions, cannot induce *de dicto/de re* ambiguities in modal contexts. One might well defend Russell by contending that his views about the logic of ordinary proper names concern extensional logic. Still, if Kripke is right he will have taught us something very important about the logic of proper names which goes beyond what the extensional logicians could reveal. Kripke further claims that his modal arguments entail that Russell's philosophical conclusions concerning problems involving proper names are mistaken. Whether that is true or not is a question which will be addressed in later chapters. For the present we will confine ourselves to the question of whether proper names induce *de dicto/de re* ambiguities in modal contexts. If they do not, as he claims, that will be reason enough for Kripke to reject a disguised description theory for modal logic.

It is obvious that there are important and close connections between proper names and descriptions: 'Aristotle' and 'the student of Plato and teacher of Alexander the Great', 'Scott' and 'the author of *Waverley*'. (One might say, in parody of Austin, that where there are names there are descriptions in the offing.) What are these connections? According to Kripke, the mistake of the classical logicians was to claim that descriptions *fix the meaning* of names; the truth is that they do not fix the meaning but only (sometimes) *fix the referent* of a name. If the name 'Aristotle' is introduced to you by saying that he was the teacher of Alexander and the student of Plato, the description merely serves to fix for you the referent of the name, it does not fix the meaning of the name or give a definition of it. Kripke's thesis here is greatly supported, I should think, by the fact that we would not ordinarily even know what was meant by "fixing the meaning," "giving a definition," or "giving a synonym" for a name. It is hard to believe that either Frege or Russell, at least when they were not being careless, ever actually claimed that descriptions did any of these things.

Kripke's principal thesis about proper names and descriptions is that *names are rigid designators* (names are always rigid designators); *descriptions generally are not rigid designators*. To say that a designator is "rigid" is to say that it denotes the same thing in every possible world in which it denotes anything at all. Obviously then, descriptions are not generally rigid designators. In this world 'the teacher of Alexander' denotes Aristotle but in other possible worlds it denotes any one of a very large number of other individuals. If this main thesis is correct, Russell's view that names are truncated descriptions is mistaken. Let us then examine this thesis. Here is Kripke's argument.

Suppose the reference of a name is given by a description or a cluster of descriptions. If the name *means the same* as that description or cluster of descriptions, it will not be a rigid designator. It will not necessarily designate the same object in all possible worlds, since other objects might have had the given properties in other possible worlds, unless (of course) we happened to use essential properties in our description. So suppose we say 'Aristotle is the greatest man who studied under Plato'. If we used that as a *definition*, the name 'Aristotle' is to mean 'the greatest man who studied under Plato'. Then of course in some other possible world that man might not have studied under Plato and some other man would have been Aristotle. If, on the other hand, we

merely use the description to *fix the referent* then that man
will be the referent of 'Aristotle' in all possible worlds. The
only use of the description will have been to pick out to which
man we mean to refer. But then we may say counterfactually
'Suppose Aristotle had never gone into philosophy at all',
we need not mean 'Suppose a man who studied with Plato,
and taught Alexander the Great, and wrote this and that,
and so on, had never gone into philosophy at all', which
might seem like a contradiction. We need only mean, 'Suppose that *that man* had never gone into philosophy at all'.[7]

The idea behind these reflections is, I believe, something like
the following. If we take the view that names have their meanings
fixed by the descriptions we sometimes use to introduce them, we
shall be unable to account for normal uses of names in the description or contemplation of counterfactual situations. This
will not be the case if we take these descriptions to be merely
fixing the referent; but it is the classical theory's contention that
descriptions do more than that, they fix the meaning of proper
names. What is involved can be expressed in terms of the *de
dicto/de re* ambiguity induced in modal contexts by descriptions.
Suppose we represent "It is necessary that the teacher of Alexander is a teacher' as

$$(7) \quad \Box T(\imath x)(Tx).$$

Then, as has been observed, this can mean

$$(8) \quad \Box[(\imath x)(Tx)]T(\imath x)(Tx),$$

which is the *de dicto* interpretation of (7) and is true. Or (7)
may mean

$$(9) \quad [(\imath x)(Tx)]\Box T(\imath x)(Tx),$$

which is the *de re* interpretation of (7) and is false. Kripke's interpretation of Russell's theory of names as a theory of the fixing
of their meanings leads him to assume that according to this
theory the descriptions which do the fixing force the *de dicto*
interpretation on modal propositions containing them. Thus he
says that if we take 'Aristotle' just to mean 'the teacher of Alexander' it will be a necessary truth that Aristotle was a teacher.

But this follows only if it follows from the assumption that 'the teacher of Alexander' fixes the meaning of 'Aristotle', that it is a necessary truth that the teacher of Alexander is a teacher. That is, to repeat, that the "fix the meaning" interpretation of Russell's theory forces the *de dicto* interpretation of modal propositions containing descriptions. It is then easy for Kripke to go on to show that Russell's theory is wrong, for surely Aristotle might not have gone into pedagogy at all, so it is just a contingent truth that Aristotle was a teacher.

This assumption that Russell's theory of descriptions forces the *de dicto* interpretation of modal propositions containing descriptions is both central to his argument against Russell and totally unjustified by Kripke. If we allow modal propositions containing descriptions to have *de re* interpretations, as surely we must, we may use them as well as names to describe counterfactual situations. Understood *de re*, it is possible that the teacher of Alexander is not a teacher (more colloquially, 'The teacher of Alexander might not have been a teacher'), just as it is possible that Aristotle is not a teacher (colloquially, 'Aristotle might not have been a teacher'). As I have said, I really do not know what it is to "fix the meaning" of a name. Thus I cannot see why Kripke should insist that if we take the "fix the meaning" interpretation of Russell's theory we cannot allow that modal propositions containing descriptions can be understood both *de dicto* and *de re*. And if these propositions can be understood *de re*, then the descriptions which they contain can be used with as much ease in the stipulation or description of counterfactual situations as names. 'Nixon might have lost the 1968 presidential election' is true, but (understood *de re*) so is 'The winner of the 1968 presidential election might not have won that election', Humphrey might have won instead.

Certainly this much can be said in favor of Kripke's view. It is, in some sense, much more natural to interpret modal propositions *de dicto*. It takes a bit of logical sophistication to see that they are susceptible of the other interpretation at all. It is also Kripke's practice always to interpret modal propositions containing names *de re*, or put less tendentiously, he does not acknowledge that names can induce the *de dicto/de re* ambiguity in modal contexts. We can use this to formulate a better way of arguing Kripke's case against Russell's description theory of names. *Names cannot be just truncated descriptions because while descriptions induce* de dicto/de re *ambiguities in modal contexts, names do not.*

Kripke's arguments against Russell, his modal arguments, depend upon the consideration that descriptions are characteristically not rigid designators. They do not hold for any name and coreferential description which is itself a rigid designator. It is of some interest, from Quine's point of view, that for any name such a rigid coreferential description can be constructed. Consider the name 'Socrates'. The required description is $(\imath x)(x=\text{Socrates})$ or, less misleadingly, $(\imath x)(x \text{ Socratizes})$. The predicate '$x$ Socratizes' was introduced by Quine for just this purpose in extensional logic and it works as well in modal logic. It is a rigid designator which designates the property of *being Socrates*. If 'Socrates', as a name, is a rigid designator, so is the predicate 'x Socratizes' which has within its extension in each possible world (in which it has anything within its extension) just that individual who is Socrates. Names, then, can by this Quinean strategem always be replaced by descriptions in modal contexts and thus eliminated via Russell's device of contextual definition. We thus arrive at the position Quine maintains for extensional logic, the elimination of all singular terms and "the primacy of predicates."

Apart from this strategy of salvaging Russell's theory by trivializing it, can it be maintained that the philosophical uses to which Russell put his theory are compatible with Kripke's modal arguments? I shall deal with this matter and Kripke's other arguments, the nonmodal arguments, against Russell's theory of names in later chapters.

IV

Is Kripke's modal thesis true? Michael Dummett has denied it and has presented some purported counterexamples. To make as strong a case against Kripke as we can we need a name such that there is some description which exhausts what we know about the bearer of that name. Such a description will be as good a candidate as we can find for a meaning fixer of the name. Dummett's candidate for such a designator is 'St. Anne'.[8] This is a good example in my case anyway because I remember the occasion upon which I learned the name. I was looking at Leonardo's famous painting of the Virgin and St. Anne and I asked my wife, "Who is St. Anne?" The reply was, "St. Anne is the mother of the Virgin Mary." To this day that is *all* I know about St. Anne. For me, the suggestion that St. Anne existed but was not the mother of Mary is simply unintelligible, as it should be in Russell's theory. Consequently, this name induces the same scope ambiguity in modal contexts as the description which "fixes its meaning" for me. Consider the statement, 'It is necessary that St. Anne is a mother' (more colloquially, 'St. Anne could not but be a mother'). It is certainly true in one sense. (I am excluding the possibility that she did not exist at all, as Kripke regularly does in these cases. The contention could be put more cautiously then as this: If St. Anne existed, she could not but have been a mother.) At the same time, of course, we must concede that St. Anne, the mother of Mary, *might* (like anyone else) have remained a virgin throughout her life and never have become a mother. So the statement

(10) It is necessary that St. Anne is a mother,

which we represent formally as

$$\Box M(s),$$

seems to admit a *de dicto* interpretation as

$$\Box[s]M(s),$$

on which interpretation it is true. (I use [s] as a scope operator for this purpose in analogy with Russell's $[(\imath x)\,(\varphi x)]$). But (10) seems equally to admit a *de re* interpretation as

$$[s]\Box M(s),$$

on which reading it is false since incompatible with

$$[s]\,\Diamond \sim M(s),$$

which is a *de re* statement saying, 'St. Anne might not have been a mother'. (She might have remained a virgin all her life.)

Other examples now come readily to mind. For me 'Homer', if he existed, is just the author of the *Iliad* and the *Odyssey*. That is all I know about him. *I* cannot make any sense of the supposition that he might have existed and not been an author, that we are simply wrong to suppose he was an author. I can, of course, consider that Homer, that is, the author of the *Iliad* and the *Odyssey*, might have gone into some other line of work (such as sailing) and consequently never have written anything. Represented formally these are just ways of exploiting the *de dicto/de re* ambiguity of

$$(11) \quad \Box A(H),$$

'Homer necessarily was an author', at least they seem to be. Interpreted *de dicto,* (11) is compatible with

$$(12) \quad \Diamond \sim A(H),$$

interpreted *de re.*

If these contentions are correct, they refute Kripke's principal thesis about proper names—that they are all rigid designators. If 'Homer' is a rigid designator, then to say that he might not have been an author ((12) above) is to say that there is a possible world in which he is not an author. But then (11) cannot be true *de dicto,* for to say that it is true is to say that in every possible world (or, more cautiously, in every possible world in which he exists), 'Homer is an author' is true. Thus to accept both (11) *de dicto* and (12) *de re* is to allow that there is a possible world in which Homer is not an author and in which 'Homer is an author' is true and this cannot be.

V

Kripke cannot admit that these names, 'St. Anne', 'Homer', or any others, do induce the *de dicto/de re* ambiguity which seems to be involved in our examples. His principal thesis about proper names—that they are all rigid designators, just is logically equivalent, in his semantics for quantified modal logic, to the thesis that they cannot induce *de dicto/de re* ambiguity. A closer look at the semantics of modal logic will clarify this point. Kripke says, "In the formal semantics of modal logic, the sense of *t* is usually taken to be the (possibly partial) function which assigns to each possible world *H* the referent of *t* in *H*. For a rigid designator, such a function is constant. . . . In the formal semantics of intensional logic, suppose we take a definite description to designate, in each world, the object satisfying the description."[9]

We will follow out these suggestions in order to get a clearer idea of the rigid/nonrigid distinction for designators. Consider a formal language with individual constants '*a*', '*b*', '*c*', in the usual style and definite descriptions. Descriptions occur in the primitive notation of the language and are not, as for Russell, introduced by contextual definitions as mere notational abbreviations. In this we follow Frege's lead. Consequently the account of the *de dicto/de re* ambiguity induced by descriptions and our account of scope ambiguity for them differs from what it would be on a Russellian formulation. On that formulation, what is at issue in these distinctions is whether the modal operator occurs outside the scope of a quantifier or within its scope when descriptions are definitionally eliminated from modal contexts. In the present account of the *de dicto/de re* distinction, what is at issue is a matter of alternative evaluation procedures for singular terms in the language with respect to the relevant set of alternative possible worlds.

Each singular term (individual constant or definite description) is evaluated by the sense functions described above. Each constant is given the *same* value (denotation) at each possible world at which it is assigned a value at all. The value of each description at each world is the unique object which satisfies the open sentence φx of the description $(\imath x)(\varphi x)$ at that world. (We need not, for our purposes, decide about the value of $(\imath x)(\varphi x)$ at a world in which there does not exist a unique object satisfying φx.) The value of $(\imath x)(\varphi x)$ will, then, generally, be different from possible world to possible world. But it need not. Formally, there is no reason why a description, like a name, should not receive the same value at each world or none at all at some or all worlds. Thus some descriptions are rigid designators. Now we can see how descriptions induce *de dicto/de re* ambiguities.

Consider $\Box\psi(\imath x)(\varphi x)$ in its *de dicto* sense, $\Box[(\imath x)(\varphi x)]\psi$ $(\imath x)(\varphi x)$. In the formal semantics of modal logic each formula is evaluated at each possible world, so let us evaluate $\Box[(\imath x)$ $(\varphi x)]\psi(\imath x)(\varphi x)$ at world **W**. First we evaluate both $(\imath x)(\varphi x)$ and ψ at **W**. The evaluation of a predicate letter assigns it an extension at each world. If the object which is the value of $(\imath x)(\varphi x)$ at **W** is a member of the extension of ψ at **W**, $\psi(\imath x)(\varphi x)$ is assigned the value True at **W**, otherwise it is assigned the value False. For any formula A, $\Box A$ is true at a world if and only if A is true at every possible world, so in order to complete the evaluation of $\Box[(\imath x)(\varphi x)]\psi(\imath x)(\varphi x)$ at **W** we need to evaluate $\psi(\imath x)(\varphi x)$ at every other possible world. The procedure followed for it at **W** is then repeated at every other possible world. If under this procedure $\psi(\imath x)(\varphi x)$ receives the value True at every possible world, then $\Box\psi(\imath x)(\varphi x)$ in its *de dicto* interpretation $\Box[(\imath x)(\varphi x)]\psi(\imath x)(\varphi x)$ is given the value True at **W**.

We contrast this with the *de re* interpretation of $\Box\psi(\imath x)(\varphi x)$ as $[(\imath x)(\varphi x)]\Box\psi(\imath x)(\varphi x)$. As above, first we evaluate $\psi(\imath x)(\varphi x)$ at **W**. But now we do not reevaluate $(\imath x)(\varphi x)$ at each alternative possible world. Instead we keep the value of $(\imath x)(\varphi x)$ fixed at its value at **W** and trace that object to each other possible world to see if it does or does not fall under the extension of ψ at each of these worlds. If it does, then $\Box\psi(\imath x)$ (φx) in its *de re* sense $[(\imath x)(\varphi x)]\Box\psi(\imath x)(\varphi x)$ is true at **W** and otherwise false. The only difference in the two evaluation procedures, *de dicto* and *de re*, is that under the first procedure the description is reevaluated at each possible world and under the second procedure the value of the description remains fixed as it is at **W**. The semantical role of the scope operator, then, is to determine whether the contained description is to be treated as a rigid or a nonrigid designator. This account is only a sketch and is, of course, otherwise incomplete. It says nothing about modal propositions involving more than one description. But it is obvious that this account can naturally be extended to these cases.

The key idea is that the scope operator may function to transform a description into a rigid designator denoting at all possible worlds the object it actually denotes.

The alternative evaluation procedures yield alternative truth-values for modal propositions containing descriptions. This is the formal account of the *de dicto/de re* ambiguity characteristically induced by descriptions in modal contexts. I say "characteristically" (not "always") because if a description is given the same value at each possible world, it does not matter for the truth-value at any world of any modal proposition containing it whether the *de re* or the *de dicto* procedure is followed for its evaluation at that world. A description which would naturally receive a constant value at each world is $(\imath x)(3 < x < 5)$ which will have the constant value 4. Such a description is a rigid designator and, for all such descriptions, the *de re/de dicto* distinction for modal propositions containing them collapses. These propositions receive the same truth-value whichever procedure of evaluation is followed.

It is clear then that since the individual constants 'a', 'b', and 'c' of our formal language are rigid designators, modal propositions containing them have the same truth-value whether the propositions are interpreted *de dicto* or *de re*. This distinction collapses for all rigid designators. (We have only sketched the argument for the simplest case where the modalized proposition is atomic, but for present purposes this is enough. Something will be said later about identity-sentences involving two designators.) This is in general not true for descriptions. A necessary and sufficient condition for any designator (individual constant or definite description) to be a rigid designator is the following, where D is an unspecified designator, $[D]$ a scope operator interpreted semantically as above, and $F(D)$ atomic:

$$\Box[D]F(D) . \equiv . [D]\Box F(D).$$

Kripke's "modal arguments" against Russell's disguised description theory of names come down to the claim that since names are always rigid designators and descriptions are not, names are not abbreviated (disguised, truncated) descriptions.

VI

What then is to be made of the examples of 'St. Anne' and 'Homer'? They appear to be cases of proper names which induce the same scope ambiguities with respect to modal operators which have been seen to be the characteristic mark of nonrigidity in designators. Can we just admit that these names are disguised descriptions, as Russell says they are? This would be to abandon Kripke's thesis in its full strength but we might still adhere to a modified version of it which says that names are characteristically rigid designators though there are some names which are not.

This alternative is really not open, because if 'Homer' is a truncated description in 'Necessarily, Homer is an author', so is it also in 'Necessarily, Homer=Homer'. This latter would then be ambiguous according to the scope accorded the description for which 'Homer' stands. To give an account of this ambiguity, we need to extend the account of the alternative evaluation procedures already given to cases in which more than one description occurs in a statement or in which a single description occurs more than once. In order to see how the extension works, let us consider the following example:

$$(13) \quad \text{Necessarily, Homer=Homer,}$$

where the name is supposed to be short for some definite description. To indicate that a description is to be evaluated according to the *de re* procedure, we will attach a subscript to it thus, $(\imath x)\,(\varphi x)_{\text{R}}$ ('R' for 'rigid'). To indicate that the description is to be evaluated according to the *de dicto* procedure, we will attach another subscript to it thus, $(\imath x)\,(\varphi x)_{\overline{\text{R}}}$ ('$\overline{\text{R}}$' for 'nonrigid'). Of the four possibilities, we need consider only two. According to the first of these, (13) is interpreted at the actual world as

$$(14) \quad \Box\,(\imath x)\,(\varphi x)_{\overline{\text{R}}}=(\imath x)\,(\varphi x)_{\overline{\text{R}}},$$

in which case it is, of course, true. It is, however, possible to interpret (13) as

$$(15) \quad \Box\,(\imath x)\,(\varphi x)_{\text{R}}=(\imath x)\,(\varphi x)_{\overline{\text{R}}}.$$

On this interpretation $(\imath x)(\varphi x)_{\mathrm{R}}$ has Homer as a fixed value—its value at the actual world. The value of $(\imath x)(\varphi x)_{\overline{\mathrm{R}}}$, however, changes from one possible world to another. Suppose that 'Homer' abbreviates 'the author of the *Iliad* and *Odyssey*'. The value of $(\imath x)(\varphi x)_{\overline{\mathrm{R}}}$ will then be not Homer, but, perhaps, Plato at some possible world. But since it is not possible that Homer= Plato, (13) interpreted as (15) is false. Moreover,

$$(16)\ \Diamond\ (\imath x)(\varphi x)_{\overline{\mathrm{R}}} \neq (\imath x)(\varphi x)_{\overline{\mathrm{R}}}$$

is true on the present interpretation. There is, however, no sense in which (13) is false, and no sense in which

$$(17)\ \Diamond\ \text{Homer} \neq \text{Homer}$$

is true. In conclusion, 'Homer' cannot be interpreted as a disguised description, for if it is, there is a sense in which (13) is false—that represented by (15), and a sense in which (17) is true—that represented by (16). But there is no sense in which (13) is false and (17) true. So 'Homer' and 'St. Anne' cannot be disguised descriptions.

Kripke employs this kind of argument repeatedly, and it is his main positive argument for the thesis that ordinary proper names are rigid designators. There is a sense in which the winner of the 1968 presidential election might not have been the winner of the 1968 election. Humphrey might have won instead. But there is no sense in which Nixon might not have been Nixon. Hence, 'Nixon' is not short for 'the winner of the 1968 presidential election'.

Of course, Kripke would deny that there is any sense in which it is necessarily true that Homer is an author, or St. Anne a mother. He might say that they are contingent statements which we know *a priori* to be true. This is a surprising turn because it has long been assumed that only necessary truths can be known *a priori* and only contingent truths known *a posteriori*. But Kripke denies both of these assumptions. It is clear that he must. If ordinary proper names are rigid designators, then all true identity-statements all of whose terms are names are necessarily true. 'Hesperus=Phosphorus' is necessarily true. But it was an empirical discovery that Hesperus=Phosphorus and not knowable *a priori*. So at least some necessary truths are knowable only *a posteriori*. It follows from this that the class of *a priori* truths is not coextensive with the class of necessary truths. But Kripke argues that there are *a priori* truths which are contingent.

The example Kripke uses is one he takes from Wittgenstein concerning the standard meter bar in Paris. Wittgenstein says, "There is one thing of which we can say neither that it is one meter long nor that it is not one meter long, and that is the standard meter in Paris."[10] Kripke objects, surely correctly, that, "This seems to be a very 'extraordinary property', actually, for any stick to have. I think he must be wrong."[11] But Kripke himself finds something extraordinary about this standard meter bar. Suppose we introduce the name 'S' by the description 'the standard meter bar'. Suppose that the length *one meter* has been *defined* to be the length of that bar S, the standard meter bar. Now Kripke says that the statement, 'S is one meter long' is true *a priori*. After all, we know that S is one meter long as a matter of our definition of 'one meter', so we know it *a priori* as we do any other statement which is true by definition. However it is a purely contingent truth that S is one meter long, because that very stick which we rigidly designate with 'S' is not one meter long in other possible worlds. On Kripke's analysis, 'S is one meter long' contains two rigid designators, 'S' and 'one meter'. The expression 'one meter' is taken to rigidly designate a length, the length which by definition is the length of S in this world; but 'one meter' designates that same length in all possible worlds, even in those in which it it is not the length of S (that is, in those worlds in which S is not one meter long). Hence 'S is one meter long' is not *de dicto* necessary.

I have devoted this attention to Kripke's treatment of the standard meter bar example because it seems to make the strongest case for distinguishing a class of statements which are *a priori* and not necessary. If a similar account can be given of the St. Anne and Homer cases, he will have protected his main thesis about proper names against the threatened counterexamples. I wish to emphasize the condition expressed in the antecedent in the preceding conditional; I doubt that it can be met. The difficulty lies in the fact that we really do not have any clear account of *a prioricity*. In what way are the St. Anne and Homer cases like that of the standard meter bar? I do not see how the cases can be made similar at all. Can it be claimed that St. Anne is a mother "by definition"? Perhaps it can be said that, in some sense, it is true that St. Anne is a mother by virtue of the definition (or meaning, or sense) of 'St. Anne', certainly not of 'mother'. But then what happens to the claim that names do not have senses? Indeed, it can appear that the appeal to a difference in extensions of the concepts of the *a priori* and the necessary, the *a posteriori* and the contingent, is only an ad hoc device for avoiding counterexamples.

VII

The theory of proper names as rigid designators is a by-product of the possible world analysis of the semantics of modal concepts. It is of interest, therefore, to observe that the possible world analysis of the propositional attitudes runs into considerable difficulty with the theory of names as rigid designators. To show this let us consider a version of Russell's puzzle which involves substitutivity not of names and descriptions as does his original version, but substitutivity of proper names instead:

(1) George IV wishes to know whether Hesperus=
Phosphorus,
(2) Hesperus=Phosphorus,
∴ (3) George IV wishes to know whether Hesperus=
Hesperus.

Where lies the fallacy, according to Kripke, which leads from the truths (1) and (2) to the false (3)? Kripke does not discuss this matter, so my question requests an attempt to use ideas Kripke does put forth in an application he does not make of them. Will the idea of names as rigid designators be of any help here? Not in an obvious way, since the notion of rigid designation is explained in terms of necessity and not of knowledge. I cannot, indeed, see how the idea of names as rigid designators can be of help with this puzzle but it does cause difficulty for another attempt to deal with it, that of Jaakko Hintikka.

Hintikka says, "My basic assumption . . . is that an attribution of any propositional attitude to the person in question involves a division of all the possible worlds . . . into two classes: into those possible worlds which are in accordance with the attitude in question and into those which are incompatible with it."[12] He goes on, "There is a sense in which in discussing a propositional attitude, attributed to a person, we can restrict our attention to those possible worlds which are in accordance with this attitude. . . . The following examples will illustrate these approximate paraphrases.

a believes that p = in all the possible worlds compatible with what a believes, it is the case that p;

a does not believe that p (in the sense 'it is not the case that a believes that p') = in at least one possible world compatible with what a believes it is not the case that p."[13]

All we have to suppose in order to see the problem raised by Kripke's treatment of proper names for Hintikka's treatment of propositional attitudes is that

(4) George IV does not believe that Hesperus= Phosphorus.

According to Hintikka, then, this says that in at least one possible world compatible with what George IV believes it is not the case that Hesperus=Phosphorus. But 'Hesperus' and 'Phosphorus' are rigid designators, hence there is no possible world in which it is not the case that Hesperus=Phosphorus. The possible worlds involved in a person's beliefs are doxastically possible alternatives to his actual belief states, that is, they are mutually compatible sets of beliefs which are each compatible with the person's actual beliefs. Hintikka's analysis requires that some of these doxastically possible worlds be metaphysically impossible, at least if George IV is not to believe that Hesperus= Phosphorus. But with this, the possible world analysis of the propositional attitudes yields a paradox.

A problem very like this one was confronted by Hintikka in the earliest presentation of his logic of knowledge and belief. His principles are applicable only to idealized knowers and believers who know all of the logical consequences of what they know or believe. In particular, then, they know and believe all logically true sentences. It is obvious why such idealization is required by the possible world analysis of the propositional attitudes. People cannot believe logical falsehoods because there are no possible worlds (compatible with everything they believe) in which they are true. One then defends this analysis of the attitudes by claiming that though the knowers and believers are idealized (logically omniscient) with respect to the content of their propositional attitudes, still the attitudes analyzed are garden variety knowledge and belief. So one more dose of the same medicine can cure the difficulty arising from the necessary truth of Hesperus=Phosphorus. What is required is further idealization. Not only must our knowers and believers be logically omniscient but metaphysically omniscient as well. They must know and believe all necessary truths. Of course, while this saves the possible world account of the propositional attitudes, it leaves us with our problem about George IV. How are we to analyze the assertion that he believes that Hesperus≠Phosphorus?

4

Individual Concepts

This chapter begins with a summary statement of the position now reached. The thesis that names are rigid designators is logically equivalent to the thesis that they do not induce *de dicto/ de re* ambiguities in modal contexts. Kripke holds that proper names lack Fregean senses and apparently thinks that this follows from the thesis that they are rigid designators. The example of The Standard Meter Bar, produced by Kripke himself, seems to be a counterexample to his own principal thesis, for it seems to be a (*de dicto*) necessity that The Standard Meter Bar is one meter long as well as a (*de re*) possibility that it might not have been that length. Dummett's case of St. Anne and the example of Homer seem to provide further (and importantly different) counter-examples. Kripke deals with the case of The Standard Meter Bar by rejecting the claim for the (*de dicto*) necessity of its one meter length. It is, he says, true *a priori* that The Standard Meter Bar is one meter long but not necessary in any sense. It is merely a contingent truth that it is that length. We naturally raise the question, 'How is contingent *a priori* truth possible?' Kripke's answer is that it is because we have stipulated by definition that the length denoted by 'one meter' is to be the length of that bar. But then, what of the St. Anne and Homer cases where no stipulative definition is involved? Kripke must abandon either the distinction between the *a priori* and the necessary, or the thesis that names are rigid designators (do not induce *de dicto/de re* ambiguity), or the thesis that they lack sense. In what follows I urge the latter course and contend that it is compatible both

66

with Kripke's views about the distinction between the modalities (necessity vs. *a prioricity*) and the principal thesis about proper names. Unless we take this course we cannot deal adequately with Kripke's own case of The Standard Meter Bar and the other apparent counterexamples to his theory. I claim that Kripke's treatment of his own case is not adequate.

One might prefer, in the face of these purported counter-examples, to drop the claim that ordinary proper names are rigid designators. This is Dummett's position, but it has a very counter-intuitive consequence. If the apparent *de dicto/de re* ambiguity in the examples of The Standard Meter Bar and St. Anne discussed in the last chapter is genuine as Dummett[1] holds it is, then 'St. Anne' is not a rigid designator and neither is 'The Standard Meter Bar' (I use capital letters to transform descriptions into names), or 'S' as Kripke calls this object, or 'Homer'. This means that there is a sense in which St. Anne might not have been St. Anne, S might not have been S, Homer not have been Homer. In accord with that sense what these names denote in the actual world is not what they denote in some other possible world. But Kripke's strongest argument for his principal thesis is that there is no sense in which St. Anne might not have been St. Anne, and so on. That is, his strongest argument for the thesis that names are rigid designators is that all true identity-statements involving names are unambiguously necessarily true. The position of the present chapter is to accept this and to then go on to give an account of the purported counterexamples which depends upon distinguishing metaphysical from epistemological modalities along Kripke's lines. The principal contention of the chapter is that this solution is available with the use of Frege's notion of sense and that Kripke was wrong to think that his principal thesis required its rejection.

I

Supposing that Kripke's modal arguments against the description theory of names are sound, I want now to deal with the question of whether he is also right to conclude, as he does, that proper names (and common names as well) do not have sense at all. "The modern logical tradition, as represented by Frege and Russell, disputed Mill on the issue of singular names, but endorsed him on that of general names. Thus *all* terms, both singular and general, have a 'connotation' or Fregean sense. More recent theorists have followed Frege and Russell, modifying their views only by replacing the notion of a sense as given by a 'cluster' of properties, only *enough* of which need apply. The present view, directly reversing Frege and Russell, *endorses* Mill's view of *singular* terms, but *disputes* his view of *general* terms."[2]

At most what has been shown by the modal arguments discussed in the last chapter is that if proper names have a sense, it cannot (generally) be expressed by some unique definite description. The principle underlying these arguments is that two coreferential singular terms cannot be identical in sense if one is a rigid designator and the other is not. This principle expresses a necessary condition for identity of sense for two designators, not a sufficient condition. Remember the Quinean strategem ("Socratizes") which generates from each proper name a definite description which is rigidly coreferential with it. We did not count the Quinean strategem as rescuing Russell's theory from Kripke's arguments but rather as trivializing Russell's theory. These were not the kinds of description Russell was thinking about. In any case, terms which are rigidly coreferential are not generally identical in sense. Consider, for example, '7+5' and '12', which rigidly designate the same number but which, according to Frege, differ in sense. But, obviously, it requires more argument to show that it follows from any of this that proper names do not have sense at all, and no such argument is to be found in Kripke's lectures. Indeed, I believe that the conclusion cannot be established and that there is no incompatibility between Frege's thesis that names have sense as well as reference and Kripke's thesis that names are rigid designators. Of course, there are other arguments (nonmodal arguments) against the description and the sense theory. We will examine these in the following chapter.

It is not difficult to see how one might arrive at the view which

Kripke holds. What explains the nonrigidity of descriptions is their sense. In each possible world the description 'the president of the United States' denotes that individual, if any, who is the president of the United States. This is transparently a case in which the sense of a designator determines its reference. It is because sense remains constant that reference varies from one possible world to another. Whatever is denoted by a description at a possible world must have certain properties. What the requisite properties are is conveyed by the sense of the description. It then appears that in order to retain rigidity of reference for a designator it must be devoid of sense, for as the referent of the designator "moves" from one possible world to another its properties change; all of them, except those which are essential to its being that individual at all. Hence none of these changing properties can be required by the senses of rigid designators. The correct conclusion seems to be that rigid designators do not have sense. Kripke so concludes.

I think that conclusion is incorrect and will now show why Kripke's claims for it are mistaken. According to Frege, the sense of a name is a mode of presentation of the referent of that name. It is "one-sided illumination" of the referent. It is unfortunate that philosophical discussions of proper names are so often concentrated on the single type of the personal proper name ('Nixon', 'Homer', 'Moses'). These discussions are also too often tied to a dichotomy between proper names and definite descriptions which is supposed to exhaust the class of singular terms. It becomes even worse when we combine these two distortions to get the view that every singular term is either a personal proper name or a definite description. This bizarre idea has never been explicitly expounded; but something very close to it seems to be implicitly accepted, considering the kinds of examples on which discussions of these topics regularly turn. But there are many kinds of singular terms which fit neither of these two categories. Consider the following: 'The Pope', '*War and Peace*', '*Tom Jones*', 'Red', 'The Holy Roman Empire', 'The Morning Star', '4+3', '4', 'France', '1413 East 57 Street', '$\emptyset$' (used as a name for the null set), 'George IV', 'St. Anne'.

In discussing the issue of whether proper names have sense (or connotation), it is a mistake to consider only personal proper names, though these seem to be the most difficult case for the sense theory. Mill used the example 'Dartmouth', the name of the English city. Mill's thesis that names have denotation without connotation would have seemed much less appealing had he attempted to argue for it using an example such as '4'.

For Frege, the notion of sense was introduced to resolve his puzzle about identity. How can informative identity-statements such as 'Hesperus=Phosphorus' differ in cognitive value from trivial identities such as 'Hesperus=Hesperus'? His answer was that 'Hesperus' and 'Phosphorus', though identical in reference, differ in sense. This notion of sense, then, has to do with what we know when we know that a proposition is true. It has to do with what we understand when we understand a sentence, and with what we have to find out in order to determine whether what a sentence says is true or not. The concept of sense is thus a *cognitive* concept. I do not see how some such notion can be dispensed with if we are to provide an account of what it is to understand the meaning of a word, or of a sentence, or to understand a language. But Kripke denies that proper names have sense and he denies that common names have sense as well. Indeed, if Kripke is right there is no role for the concept of sense to play at all. How, then, can Kripke deal with Frege's problem? He tells us that 'Hesperus' and 'Phosphorus' are rigid designators and it follows from this that if 'Hesperus=Phosphorus' is true, it is a necessary truth. Now, of course, 'Hesperus=Hesperus' is also a necessary truth. How, having denied that names have sense, can Kripke account for the difference in cognitive value of the two sentences? Kripke tells us that 'Hesperus=Phosphorus' is not only necessarily true, it is also an *a posteriori* truth, one which could only be known and discovered empirically. Suppose we put ourselves in the position of a person who, not knowing the facts, is at the stage of wondering whether Hesperus=Phosphorus, and who then sets about to find out. He must, of course, know what it is that he wants to know. We can give an account of this in terms of the Fregean concept of sense, but first for some background.

Suppose that our inquirer (let him be Bernard J. Ortcutt) is shown a planet in the early evening hours and told that it is called 'Hesperus'. Let us suppose that this is the way the name 'Hesperus' is acquired by him. We may say, as Kripke does, that in this ostensive act the reference of the name has been fixed for Ortcutt. But note that the sense of the name 'Hesperus' has also been fixed by the act of ostension, for Ortcutt has acquired a criterion of identification for Hesperus. That is, the act of ostension has given Ortcutt a means to pick out (or recognize) the planet again under similar circumstances. Acquiring a name consists, in part at least, in acquiring a criterion of identification for its referent. The criterion which is associated with the name in our case by the ostensive act is just what Frege means by the sense of the name. The fixing of the reference of the name 'Hesperus' can be successfully accomplished only by associating a criterion of identification for Hesperus with that name. Another way to see this is to remind ourselves that the act of pointing to the planet while saying "That is called 'Hesperus'" (the ostensive defining of 'Hesperus') is a linguistic act which Ortcutt must understand if the act is to be successful. He must understand, among other things, that he is to project his line of sight from the shoulder through the index finger to the target of the ostension if he is to acquire the intended referent. It is only because he grasps the sense of the words uttered in those circumstances that the ostensive definition succeeds. And what then has occurred is that 'Hesperus' has been given a sense, and thereby a reference for Ortcutt.

Now let us suppose that Ortcutt, under quite different circumstances (for example, it is dawn rather than evening) is told that yonder planet is 'Phosphorus'. Let us further suppose that this is his introduction to that name, that he is now acquiring it for the first time. In acquiring this name, Ortcutt has acquired a new concept (an "individual concept") or sense and another criterion of identification for the same planet. It is obvious that he can possess these two (individual) concepts without knowing that they are concepts of the same object. He has acquired the senses of the names 'Hesperus' and 'Phosphorus' without realizing that

71

these senses are "modes of presentation" of the same referent. But having acquired the names and thereby the individual concepts (or senses) associated with them he is now in a position to understand or ask the question 'Is Hesperus=Phosphorus?' He is in a position to wonder whether these two concepts are concepts of the same object. He cannot discover that they are by sitting up all night with his eyes fixed on the planet, because it disappears from view before dawn and appears in the morning in another part of the heavens. So inferences have to be made to secure the identification. That is why the identification was not made from the start. But once Ortcutt does discover (either by himself or from others) the identity, his discovery will be that the criterion of identification associated by him with 'Hesperus' and that associated by him with 'Phosphorus' pick out the same object, Venus. Acquiring the sense of 'Hesperus' gives Ortcutt the ability to reidentify an object (Venus) under certain circumstances, the circumstances in which that name was introduced to him. He may be able to do that without being able to reidentify that same planet under quite other circumstances. Thus it is an empirical discovery that the objects he identifies under these very different circumstances are one and the same. His discovery is that two (individual) concepts are concepts of the same object. Thus what Ortcutt discovers is not merely a fact about words or names. 'Hesperus= Phosphorus' does not mean that 'Hesperus' denotes the same object as 'Phosphorus'. One could know the latter without knowing that Hesperus=Phosphorus. But one cannot know this without knowing that the individual concept Hesperus and the individual concept Phosphorus are concepts of the same object. Think of a sense as a road. Two roads may lead to the same destination without our knowing it, even though we are acquainted with the roads. It can be a discovery that they both go to the same place. But we cannot fail to know that each road goes where it goes wherever that is. Just so, Ortcutt cannot fail to know that the (individual) concept or sense associated by him with 'Hesperus' cannot be a concept of two objects, so he knows *a priori* that 'Hesperus=Hesperus'. Kripke's problem is to explain how necessary truths *a posteriori* are possible, and in abandoning the no-

72

tion of sense he seems to have abandoned the only available the-
.ory which can provide an answer.

One might object that the example just given begs the question
by using names which acquire a sense in virtue of their etymology.
'Hesperus' connotes evening and 'Phosphorus' light and therefore morning. It will therefore be helpful to offer another example, which Dummett gives from Frege's correspondence, which
is not subject to this objection and is similar to one made famous
later by Quine.

> Frege imagines a traveller going into an unexplored region
> and descrying a large mountain on the southern horizon,
> to which he gives the name 'Alfa'. Some twenty years later,
> another explorer spots a large mountain on his north-
> western horizon, and calls it 'Ateb'. The stories of both
> travellers receive considerable publicity, and both moun-
> tain-names pass into common use: but it is many years
> until these regions are more systematically explored and
> mapped, and when this is done, it is discovered, to the sur-
> prise of all, that the two explorers had been viewing the
> same mountain from different angles; owing to errors on
> their part in estimating distances, plotting their positions,
> etc., this had never been envisaged as a possibility. It is
> thus a geographical discovery that Alfa and Ateb are one
> and the same mountain.[3]

Dummett adds the observation that once the discovery is made,
either one name will be dropped, or both will be used synonymously.[4]

That the sense of a name conveys a criterion of identification
for its referent is emphasized by Dummett. Is this incompatible
with the thesis that names are rigid designators? I do not see
how it can be. Names are rigid designators because they pick
out the same referent in every possible world. Objects change
their properties from one possible world to the next. Nixon, for
example, is a Democrat in some possible world. But note that
in order to understand this last assertion we must have acquired
the name 'Nixon' and with it some criterion of identification for
him. It is Nixon, the individual of whom we possess this concept,

of whom it is being said that he might have been a Democrat, or a Communist, or a philosopher, or whatever. The fact that he has different properties in different possible worlds does not entail that the sense of 'Nixon' changes as I describe one counterfactual situation after the other. On the contrary, the fact that we understand each of these counterfactual statements to be about the same man, Nixon, entails that the sense of 'Nixon' remains constant from one counterfactual statement to the other. A rigid designator is one whose sense is such that it is a concept of the same object in every possible world in which that object exists.

II

Many have thought that whether right or wrong about proper names, Mill was surely right to ascribe connotation to common names such as 'man', 'horse', 'gold'. Kripke thinks that Mill was wrong about this and that Mill's common names ("natural kind terms") are like proper names both in being rigid designators and in that they do not have sense. Here he agrees with Frege in offering a unified account of both kinds of names. But it is of interest to inquire why Mill's original division should have seemed right in the first place to many who wrote after him. The idea seems to be that if we grasp the meaning (sense, connotation) of a natural kind term such as 'cat', what we have acquired is a criterion of identification for animals of that kind. Knowing the meaning of 'cat' consists, in part, in being able to identify some object as a cat. It is a question of fit. Does this animal fit the concept Cat? But then why does a quite parallel account not apply to proper names, including personal proper names? We are not in a position to determine whether or not Nixon is in the next room unless we know such things as that Nixon is a person and not, for example, a cat. In other words, we must know what the truth-conditions are for the sentence 'Nixon is in the next room' and this involves knowing the sense of 'Nixon'. So a quite parallel account is correct for both proper names and common names—an account which ascribes sense and reference to both.

Perhaps another source of difficulty over this matter is that it sounds odd to speak of the "meaning" of proper names such as 'Napoleon' (but not odd at all to speak of the meaning of '4'). But what importance is this supposed to have? To be sure, it does not sound odd to speak of the meaning of 'cat'. These seem to be facts about the word 'meaning', a difficult word to understand, no doubt. But there is no reason to conflate this vague concept of "meaning" with Frege's sense, which is a notion with considerably more structure and part of a rather elaborately articulated theory. I do not know what else to say about the repeated observation that "We do not, in ordinary language, talk about the 'meanings' of proper names."

I have found in discussing this subject that objection to the position I am defending is often given something like the following form: "If proper names have sense why can their sense not be expressed by some definite description or other? Why, for example, can you not *say* what the sense of 'Nixon' is?" But this is a rather odd requirement. Consider first common names which generally have been thought to have sense, or names of qualities, or tastes, or smells. How do you tell someone the sense of the word 'yellow' or 'sweet'? For that matter, how do you tell someone the sense of the word 'game'? The example, of course, recalls Wittgenstein's famous discussion of games in introducing his notion of "family resemblances." He was arguing that a term such as 'game' does not have "sharp outlines," cannot be given a definition in terms of necessary and sufficient conditions which will decide concerning every case whether or not it is correctly called a game. He argued that there was no common characteristic possessed by all games and by games alone. Wittgenstein wanted to make the point that this did not mean that the word 'game' was without a use for us. Wittgenstein's target in these discussions is the Platonic idea that when a number of things are all called by the same name, 'man', or 'bed', or 'justice', it is because there is something they all have in common—'humanity' or 'bedness', and so on. He is also connecting this idea with Frege's idea that concepts must have sharp boundaries; that there cannot be borderline cases of genuine concepts. But none of what Wittgenstein has to say about family resemblances is really incompatible with Frege's sense/reference distinction as applied either to proper names, to common names such as 'game', or to names for natural kinds such as 'gold'. To say that 'game' is a family resemblance term is just a way of characterizing its sense.

III

Kripke argues that natural kind terms such as 'gold' are also rigid designators and seems to believe that this alone establishes his thesis that they do not have sense. As in the case of proper names the conclusion does not follow, but it will be instructive to look closer at Kripke's argument in the case of natural kind terms to see why he thinks this conclusion does follow, because it contains the same mistake which leads to the wrong conclusion about proper names. Kripke discusses a quotation from Paul Ziff. "I say 'The word 'tiger' has meaning in English'. . . . If I am then asked 'What is a tiger?' I might reply 'A tiger is a large carnivorous quadrupedal feline, tawny yellow in color with blackish transverse stripes and white belly' (derived from the entry under 'tiger' in the *Shorter Oxford English Dictionary*)."[5] Kripke goes on, "And now someone says 'You have just said what the word 'tiger' means in English.' And Ziff asks 'Is that so?' and he says correctly, 'I think not'. His example is 'Suppose in a jungle clearing one says 'Look, a three-legged tiger!': must one be confused? The phrase 'a three-legged tiger' is not a *contradictio in adjecto*. But if 'tiger' in English meant, among other things, either quadruped or quadrupedal, the phrase 'a three-legged tiger' could only be a *contradictio in adjecto*."[6] Kripke thinks that all of this is correct, as I do. What does the example show? It shows that "if it is part of the concept of tiger that a tiger has four legs, there couldn't be a three-legged tiger."[7] Kripke then goes on to add that it is not even a contradiction to suppose that we might discover that tigers never have four legs. The explorers who attributed this property to the tiger might all have been suffering from an optical illusion and the animals they saw were from a three-legged species. "Would we then say that there turned out to be no tigers after all? I think we would say that in spite of the optical illusion which had deceived the explorers, tigers in fact have three legs."[8] Then Kripke seems to generalize that if it is not "part of the concept" of being a tiger that an animal be three-legged then none of the other characteristics listed in the dictionary entry are part of the concept of being a tiger either. "Mill says that *all* 'general' names are connotative; such a predicate as 'human being' is defined as the conjunction of certain properties which give necessary and sufficient conditions for humanity—rationality, animality, and certain physical features."[9] Kripke explains that, "My own view . . . regards Mill as more-or-less right about 'singular' names, but wrong about 'general' names. *Perhaps* some 'general' names ('foolish', 'fat', 'yellow') express properties. In a significant sense, such general names as 'cow' and 'tiger' do not. . . . Certainly "cow' and 'tiger' are *not* short for the conjunction of properties a dictionary would take to define them as Mill thought."[10]

Kripke then goes on to argue for his view that terms such as 'gold', 'cow', and 'tiger', natural kind terms, are rigid designators just as are "singular" names. We can use these terms to stipulate counterfactual situations, for example 'Gold might not have been yellow', 'Cows might not have been four-legged', and so on. The idea is that if words of this kind required the possession of these properties by their definitions, the use of these terms for the stipulation of counterfactual situations would involve the construction of contradictory descriptions, of cows which are not cows, gold which is not gold, and so on. But if this is the argument, it does not show that natural kind terms lack sense. It is precisely because such terms have sense that we can understand which counterfactual situation is being stipulated. It is that which falls under the concept Gold which is supposed not to be yellow, and so on. The sense of the words 'gold', 'cow', 'tiger' includes the identity-conditions which we invoke when we classify things as being of these kinds.

Kripke's thesis applies not only to terms for natural kinds; it is far wider. "This conclusion holds for certain for various species names, whether they are count nouns, such as 'cat', 'tiger', 'chunk of gold', or mass terms such as 'gold', 'water', 'iron pyrites'. It also applies to certain terms for natural phenomena, such as 'heat', 'light', 'sound', 'lightning', and presumably, suitably elaborated, to corresponding adjectives—'hot', 'loud', 'red'."[11] The conclusion is that terms of all of these kinds which are not proper names are like proper names both because they are rigid designators and because they lack "connotation or Fregean sense." What is the argument for these conclusions? It is contained in the following statements: "We use 'gold' as a term for a certain *kind* of thing. Others have discovered this kind of thing and we have heard of it. We thus as part of a community of speakers have a certain connection between ourselves and a certain kind of thing. The kind of thing is *thought* to have certain identifying marks. Some of these marks may not really be true of gold. We might discover that we are wrong about them."[12] Further, there might be a kind of thing which did have all of these identifying marks without being gold. Iron pyrites or fool's gold is such a kind of thing. Now what we say of iron pyrites is not that it really is gold because it possesses the identifying properties which we originally used to pick out gold, but that we were wrong to take the properties which we origially used to pick out gold as being either necessary or sufficient for a substance being gold. "We can say this not because we have changed the *meaning* of the term 'gold' and thrown in some other criteria which distinguished gold from pyrites. . . . We *discovered* that certain properties were true of gold in addition to the initial identifying marks by which we identified it. These properties, being characteristic of gold and not true of iron pyrites, show that the fool's gold is not in fact gold."[13]

The argument is that the identifying properties which we use to pick out gold do not "fix the meaning" (connotation, sense) of the term 'gold', they only fix the reference. In fact the term 'gold' does not have a meaning (connotation, sense). We cannot take the sense of the term 'gold' to be a criterion of identification for things of this kind because this criterion does not enable us to distinguish between gold and iron pyrites. Kripke has clearly hit on something of great importance here. How can we account for this case along Fregean lines? The clue is given by Kripke himself. Natural kind terms are rigid designators. They denote kinds, the same kinds in all possible worlds. The sense of the kind-term is a concept of the reference of the term. This accounts for our ability to understand the assertions that gold might not have been yellow, tigers might not have had stripes, and so on. We keep our grip on the kind as it moves through metaphysical space from one possible world to another, by means of the kind-name, which rigidly denotes the kind throughout these metaphysical metamorphoses.

Further, the concept of sense is needed to give an account of what we know when we know the meaning of sentences using natural kind terms. The sentence 'Gold is to be found in those hills' says something different from the sentence 'Copper is to be found in those hills'. In Frege's terms they express different thoughts. A full declarative sentence names a truth-value and the sense of the sentence (the thought) conveys the conditions under which that truth-value is the true. "The names, whether simple or themselves composite, of which the name of a truth-value consists, contribute to the expression of the thought, and this contribution of the individual component is its *sense*."[14] So the difference in the truth-conditions of the two sentences mentioned above results from the difference in sense between 'gold' and 'copper'. Again, the difference in cognitive value between the informative identity 'Gold=the element with atomic number 79' and the trivial 'Gold=gold' is to be explained by the difference in sense of the designators involved.

What then shall we say about the example of iron pyrites which, to the naked eye, have all of the identifying properties of gold? The sense of 'gold' is a criterion of identification for the kind gold. The sense of 'the element with atomic number 79' provides another criterion of identification for the same kind. What is to be concluded from this example of a kind which agrees in all of its external appearances with gold but which is not in fact gold is just that the sense of 'gold' is not such that what looks like gold is gold. The criterion of identification for the correct application of 'gold' is not exhausted by appearances, especially appearances to the naked and untrained eye.

As long as people have used the term 'gold', surely it has been realized that distinguishing this kind from other metals might involve some sophisticated tests only capable of being performed by experts. In any case, the sense which we give to that term does not restrict our criterion of identification to unsophisticated phenomenal tests (look, feel, taste, and so on). I believe that it is part of our concept of natural kinds that their phenomenal traits are due to underlying structures, atomic or genetic structures, and it is part of the sense of natural kind terms that the conditions for their correct application are not entirely matters of surface appearance. Surface appearance is normally a safe indicator that the essential underlying structure is present, but not always as, for example, with fool's gold. This just shows that underlying structures, unobservable to the naked eye, are involved in the criteria of identification for natural kinds and hence involved in the very sense of names for natural kinds; it does not show that such names lack sense.

Suppose that astronauts land on Mars and find a substance there that fills the lakes and runs in the streams and falls from the clouds and looks, tastes, and feels exactly like water. But chemical analysis reveals that it does not have the structure of H_2O.[15] We would deny that this stuff is water. Suppose that these astronauts also found creatures that looked exactly like tigers, behaved like tigers, had the internal structure of tigers (stomach, lungs, kidneys, and so on); I think that nevertheless we would deny that these creatures were tigers. Why? Because tigers are a kind all the members of which have a common origin. That is part of the sense of the term 'tiger'. Since those creatures on Mars could not have the same origin as our tigers they cannot be tigers. If the astronauts did find a substance with the structure H_2O, they would have discovered water on Mars. So we can say now that there may be water on Mars but that there certainly are no tigers or humans.[16] What the examples show is something about the sense of kind-names (the criteria of identification for kinds). In particular, the examples show that the sense of such terms does not merely involve phenomenal properties detectable by the naked and untutored senses.

In this respect they can be contrasted with other "common names" which are names for "conventional" kinds such as 'bed', 'lamp', 'house'. These are names for artifacts (non-natural kinds) and criteria for their identification do not invoke underlying structure as in the case of gold, or origin, as with tigers. Still, even these criteria are not purely a matter of phenomenal appearance. What looks like a bed, and feels and tastes and smells like one, and is indistinguishable by the senses from a real bed, might not really be a bed. Suppose such things were found on Mars with no evidence of the existence of rational creatures of any kind inhabiting that planet. Suppose further that these objects just grow on Mars as do our trees. What makes it wrong to call them 'beds' is that it is part of the sense of the term that beds are objects made with a certain purpose. If there are no creatures on Mars who have this purpose, these objects cannot satisfy the identification-condition for beds. Phenomenal qualities are all that are relevant in the case of names for colors, smells, and tastes. There is no "fool's red" or "fool's sweet" as there is fool's gold. But what this shows is just that criteria of identification are sometimes purely phenomenal and sometimes a mixture of purely observational qualities with other characteristics of a more theoretical nature. Identification by phenomenal properties is normally all that is required for everyday practical purposes. We are, however, fully prepared to be corrected by experts when they exist, as with gold and jewelry; and the possibility of correction of identifications based on appearance is built into the very sense of these words.

It may be objected that people used the term 'gold' and names for other natural kinds long before anything was known about atomic theory or genetics. But I am not talking about the sense of these terms for people living that long ago, I am talking about our use of these terms. It may be that they did use these terms with different senses. I do not care to reach a decision about this at this point. I only wish to point out that the senses of words can change with increase in knowledge. I suspect, however, that names for natural kinds have for a long time involved reference to some kind of underlying and unobservable structures (or origins) in their sense. That is what makes it part of the sense of these names that the kinds they name are "natural."

IV

We can deploy the idea of individual concepts to provide an account of the St. Anne case, the Homer case, and The Standard Meter Bar case which allows us to resolve the difficulties they seem to present without abandoning the thesis that these names are rigid designators. The difficulty is that these names seem to induce the same *de dicto/de re* ambiguity as that typically produced by definite descriptions in modal contexts. Kripke's solution to this difficulty is to invoke a division between metaphysical and epistemological modalities. 'The Standard Meter Bar is one meter long' is *a priori* true but metaphysically contingent. This can seem an ad hoc maneuver to save the thesis that names are rigid designators. Are we merely trading ambiguity of scope (*de dicto* vs. *de re*) for ambiguity of modality (*a priori* truth vs. *de dicto* necessity)? This is more unsatisfactory when no genuine account is offered of *a prioricity*. Indeed, in his review of Kripke's "Identity and Necessity," Quine charges Kripke with doing precisely this. He says, "Kripke sums up these matters in other words: genuine names he calls *rigid designators,* necessity *de re* he calls *metaphysical necessity,* and necessity *de dicto* he calls *a priori truth.* He furnishes examples to make us feel at home with the circumstance that necessary truths (*de re*) can be mooted (being contingent *de dicto*)." He then concludes, "I can read Kripke gratefully as abetting my effort to show what a tangled web the modalist weaves."[17] Quine is accusing Kripke of renaming *de dicto* necessity "*a priori* truth" and of doing nothing more. In order to repel this charge, an account must be given as to how it is possible to know contingent truths *a priori*.

Kripke does offer an account of The Standard Meter Bar case, but one which is incomplete. The explanation is that, after all, we have stipulated by definition that that bar is to be the standard of the meter length. This means, in our terms, that the designator 'one meter' has been given a certain sense. That sense, "by definition," is a concept of the length of the standard meter bar in the actual world. The sense of 'one meter' is not a concept of the bar, but of its length. The notion of sense again provides what is missing in Kripke's account. How, according to him, do we get from the stipulation that one meter is to be the length of that bar to the truth of the assertion that the bar is a meter long? There is nothing in Kripke's conceptual apparatus to explain this. If the statement 'The Standard Meter Bar is one meter long' is true (and *a priori*), then what it says is the case, that is, its truth-conditions obtain, and, if Kripke is right, we know *a priori* that they obtain. Here is where the notion of sense comes in. The sense of 'one meter' is such that the criterion of identification for that length has been stipulated to be that of that bar—has been stipulated to be the length of that bar, not the bar. Hence we know *a priori* that the bar is one meter long.

Similar accounts can be given for the St. Anne and Homer cases. There is a sense in which St. Anne could not but have been a mother and Homer an author. It is true *a priori* for me that St. Anne is a mother, because having acquired the name 'St. Anne' by means of the single definite description 'the mother of Mary', I cannot make intelligible to myself the supposition that though she exists, she is not a mother. This is, of course, compatible with the view that it is a contingent truth that St. Anne is a mother. It is, after all, a contingent truth about any mother that she is a mother. So we can safely explain the apparent *de dicto/de re* ambiguities induced by these names, which threaten their rigid designator status, as really differences of modality, epistemic and metaphysical.

I am not claiming that in cases in which we acquire the sense of a name with a single definite description that the sense acquired is the same as that of the description. In fact that cannot be the case, for it is *de dicto* necessary that the mother of Mary is a mother, and the author of the *Iliad* and the *Odyssey* an author.

Thus if the sense of the name 'St. Anne' is identical with the sense of 'the mother of Mary' it would follow that it is also necessary *de dicto* that St. Anne is a mother, and this I have been at some pains to deny. The situation is that the name gains only part of its sense from the description which introduces it to us. Another constituent of its sense accrues to it solely by virtue of the fact that it is a proper name. It is by virtue of this constituent of its sense that we know that any proper name is a rigid designator. Thus, in our case of 'St. Anne', which we suppose to have been acquired by us with the use of the single definite description 'the mother of Mary', the name and the description are still not identical in sense for us. We could not have acquired the use of this name with the aid of that description unless we already recognized the term as a name. Personal proper names characteristically lack the complexity of syntactic and semantic structure which always belongs to definite descriptions. It is this which has led to the mistaken view that they lack sense altogether. The name 'St. Anne' does have a semantic complexity which 'Homer' and 'Moses' lack. But it is part of the sense of any proper name that it designates rigidly. We know this about a term as soon as we recognize it as a name. We may learn what a name denotes by means of a definite description which fixes a criterion of identification for the referent of the name, as in the case of 'St. Anne'. Still, the sense of 'St. Anne' is not the same as the sense of 'the mother of Mary', and the same holds generally for names which we acquire by means of some one definite description such as (perhaps) 'Homer'.

V

The example given above of the introduction of the names 'Hesperus' and 'Phosphorus' through acts of ostension has a special simplicity which makes it apt as an illustration of my thesis. The ostensive introduction of a name ('That is called 'Hesperus'') associates both a sense and a reference with the name, 'Hesperus'. How could a referent be associated with the name ostensively without, at the same time, giving the name a sense which presents that referent? What is it for me to have learned the reference of the name 'Hesperus' in the act of ostension? I have acquired a criterion of identification for Hesperus which I can exercise in my use of that term.

What then are we to make of the distinction, so prominent in Kripke's lectures, between the "fixing of the reference" and the "fixing of the meaning" of a designator? If we confine ourselves to situations in which a designator is being introduced, then Kripke is wrong to suppose that one can fix the reference without fixing the meaning (sense) of a term. If I explain to a pupil that 'π' denotes C/D, then I have given both sense and reference to 'π'. If I explain that 'St. Anne' is the mother of Mary and this is the first time you have ever heard the name, then you acquire not only a reference but a sense of that term as well. But if you already have acquired the use of a name, for example, 'Venus', and have therefore already associated some sense with it, when you are told that Venus=the morning star, you do not acquire another sense for 'Venus' (that would just render the name ambiguous). What you learn is that the sense you already associate with 'Venus' is a concept of a certain object. It is the same object as that of which the sense which you associate with 'the morning star' is also a (individual) concept. That is why the identity-statement conveys genuine information for you, unlike the trivial 'Venus=Venus'.

But what about names not acquired through acts of ostension? Here the picture is less clear. The case of 'St. Anne' is again not typical because we were imagining the situation to be one in which the name is first acquired. But take a name like 'Moses'. Of course, there was an occasion on which each of us first acquired the name. But that occasion is, for most of us, now long forgotten. Maybe what we heard then was that Moses led the Israelites out of Egypt. But subsequently we learn (or think we learn) all sorts of additional facts concerning him. Perhaps we read Freud and come to believe that he was an Egyptian rather than a Jew. It is not at all realistic to suppose that the sense originally associated with the name 'Moses' remains fixed, and that all the new information acquired about him and expressed in identity-statements involving 'Moses' just presents additional concepts of the same object in the manner of the simple example of 'Hesperus=Phosphorus' given above.

A more realistic picture is that presented by Wittgenstein.

> If one says 'Moses did not exist', this may mean various things. It may mean: the Israelites did not have a *single* leader when they withdrew from Egypt—or: their leader was not called Moses—or: there cannot have been anyone who accomplished all that the Bible relates of Moses—. . . But when I make a statement about Moses—am I always ready to substitute some *one* of these descriptions for 'Moses'? I shall perhaps say: by 'Moses' I understand the man who did what the Bible relates of Moses, or at any rate, a good deal of it. But how much? Have I decided how much must be proved false for me to give up my proposition as false? Has the name 'Moses' got fixed and unequivocal use for me in all possible cases?[18]

Let us compare this with relatively simple examples of The Standard Meter Bar and St. Anne. We have stipulated that the length one meter is to be the length of that bar. Hence we know *a priori* that it is one meter long. Supposing that all we know about St. Anne is that she is the mother of Mary, then we know that *a priori* as well. But what about Moses? Do we know *a priori* at least that he was a Jew? Or that he was taken out of the Nile by Pharaoh's daughter? Or that he received the commandments on Mt. Sinai? I would say that we do not. And the reason is what Wittgenstein says it is. The name 'Moses' does not have a fixed and unequivocal sense for us in all possible cases. "Is it not the case that I have, so to speak, a whole series of props in readiness, and am ready to lean on one if another should be taken from under me and vice versa?"[19] Under these circumstances, and they are typical of a large class of words (not only proper names), the notion of *a priori* truth becomes impossible to apply.

What then of the individual concept Moses? What is the criterion of identification for Moses? The picture which Wittgenstein presents of this matter is the correct one. In our actual use of language we do not employ an unequivocal and fixed criterion of identification for Moses, any unequivocal and fixed sense of that name. That does not mean that the name 'Moses' is useless for these everyday purposes of communication. It does mean that the truth-conditions for statements about him are not exact and that there is no clear line between what we know *a priori* about him (by virtue of our concept of Moses) and what is known only *a posteriori,* if at all.

Frege's theory, according to which each name expresses a unique and precisely specifiable sense and every concept has "sharp boundaries" which exclude borderline cases, abstracts from actual language in much the same way that a scientific theory abstracts from actual conditions in the world and uses constructs like frictionless media, perfectly rigid bodies, perfectly flat surfaces. Frege's immediate purpose was to provide an account of the language of arithmetic, and here the ideal conditions of this theory are in fact realized. There is no element of vagueness in the sense of '4', nor are there borderline cases of natural numbers.

In our actual use of language we tolerate (and even welcome) vagueness and imprecision. We use words with only the faintest idea of what they mean, and it does not matter at all. Two cases are to be distinguished. One is that of words which do not have a precise sense in the language. The other is that of words which do have a (more or less) precise sense, though we use them without knowing what it is, either because we have forgotten or because we never knew. An example of the latter kind (for me) is the term 'cashier's check'. I have used those words on many occasions. I have been told that something must be paid for with a cashier's check. I go to the bank and purchase one (I ask for and obtain one) and carry through my business with it. I do not know the definition of 'cashier's check' or 'North Pole' or 'red blood cell', or 'county', or 'gravity', and so on. But that does not interfere with my successful use of these words. I know that the words do have (more or less) precise meanings and that I can, if necessary, find out what these are. Frege's picture, according to which the sense of words is grasped by anyone who speaks

87

and understands the language, is a highly idealized model of actual practice. But the case of 'Moses' is different from that of 'cashier's check' in that not only do I not attach a precise sense to the name, it does not have one. That is the situation Wittgenstein is depicting. "If I say 'Moses did not exist' this may mean various things."

For certain purposes this prevalent absence of precision may be intolerable, for example, in the law. Or we may wish to decide the question of whether there was a historical Homer, or Moses. Then the criterion of identification associated with these names will have to be tightened if a decision is to be reached. Just so, in the law, terms such as 'negligence', 'consent', 'fraud', and so on must be given precise sense if disputes are to be resolved. Frege's theory of language and in particular his concepts of sense and reference provide theoretical concepts with which to give an account of what is going on in these cases. If vagueness and imprecision are intolerable in certain circumstances, they can be eliminated. Suppose it becomes important to decide about the historicity of Homer, or Moses. Criteria of identification will have to be fixed before these questions can rationally be investigated and answered. As this tightening occurs, our language (or that area of it relevant to our investigation) will come more and more to approach the Fregean model of a perfect language or another very like it.

The classification of identities as informative or trivial is unrealistic for these reasons. It is, by now, difficult to believe that 'Hesperus=Phosphorus" or 'Cicero=Tully' is indeed more informative than 'Hesperus=Hesperus' or 'Cicero=Cicero'. The former assertions were informative when we first learned them but by now they are not. These tired examples are used over and over in discussions of these topics just because it is difficult to find examples of objects which have more than one proper name. Frege resorted to imagination in order to come up with his example of 'Alfa' and 'Ateb'. This mountain had two names as a result of a mistake, and the same applies to the case of Venus. Once the mistake is discovered and the identification made, there is no longer any reason for the multiplicity of names to be retained.

The two names had different senses before the discovery of the error; that explains the cognitive value of the sentence expressing the identification. After the discovery that Cicero is Tully and Ateb is Alfa, the senses of the two names tend to merge into one. It becomes pointless to retain them both and one or the other will tend to fall into disuse. There is no point in an object having more than one proper name and there is a good reason against it in the avoidance of confusion and misunderstanding. These observations do not, of course, apply to alternative descriptions denoting the same object. They do retain distinct senses. This points to an important distinction in the roles of names and descriptions in language. It is not a reason for denying that names have sense.

VI

It may occur to some that Kripke has provided a place for the concept of sense in his formal semantics for modal logic. For each type of designator there is a function which assigns it an extension in every possible world and these functions are taken by him to be the sense of these designators.[20] This gives us a concept of sense which has little in common with Frege's concept, and for the sake of clarity it would be better to call it the 'intension' of the term as Carnap, who first presented the idea, generally does.[21] It is because these intensions have no relation to what it is that we know when we know the meaning of an expression that they cannot be taken as Fregean senses. Carnap adopted an extended relation of logical equivalence as his criterion of identity for intensions of designators. As a consequence, all logically equivalent sentences have the same intension. (Following Frege, he takes full sentences to be a type of designator.) But logically equivalent sentences are, in general, certainly different in Fregean sense. Otherwise it would be impossible to explain how we can understand these sentences without knowing their truth-values. Again, for Carnap the two individual designators of a logically true identity have the same intension. If this intension is taken as the sense of these designators, logically true identities involving two designators all come to have the same sense as the trivial identities which take each of these designators twice over. Frege's concept of sense was introduced precisely to avoid this paradox.

It thus becomes impossible to relate the Carnap-Kripke concept of intension to knowledge of meanings at all, and consequently I find it impossible to figure out what role it is supposed to play in a model of language. We have seen that, according to Kripke, true identities all of whose terms are rigid designators are necessarily true. Whatever denotation is assigned to 'Hesperus' in a possible world is also assigned to 'Phosphorus'. Thus they both have the same intension. Then how can it be an *a posteriori* truth that Hesperus=Phosphorus and an *a priori* truth that Hesperus=Hesperus? These modalities are epistemic rather than metaphysical. The Carnap-Kripke concept of an intension simply fails to connect with any cognitive role for meanings, for surely it is a difference in what we know when we understand what a sentence means which determines whether it is knowable *a priori* or *a posteriori*.

Granted that meaning and sense are correlative with knowledge, with what we know when we understand an expression of our language, we can now attempt to say more precisely what a knowledge of sense consists in. The sense of a declarative sentence embodies the truth-conditions for the sentence. What then is it to know these truth-conditions? Senses generally embody criteria for recognition of objects. To know the truth-conditions of a declarative sentence is to have a criterion for recognition of a truth-value. The sense of a sentence, its truth-conditions, embodies a mode of presentation of a truth-value or way in which a truth-value is given. We can understand sentences (know their truth-conditions) without, however, knowing their truth-value. So what needs explaining is how a sentence manages to present its truth-value without our necessarily coming to know what it is merely by virtue of our understanding the meaning of the sentence.

We face a parallel problem with individual designators. The sense of an individual designator embodies a recognition condition for its referent which we grasp in understanding the designator. Still we may grasp the sense of a designator and hence, in some sense, grasp its referent, without knowing what it is. I am afraid I cannot do much more with this than to illustrate these theses in a convincing manner, and to clear away some of the roadblocks in the way to their acceptance. The problem lies in the unclarity in the notion of knowing what (or who) something is. Do you know who the mayor of Rome is if you answer in response to the question that he is the person who won the last mayoral election? That is a correct description of this person, but it would not be taken as a reason for saying of someone that he knows who the mayor of Rome is. The truth-value of Goldbach's hypothesis is the truth-value thereof that every even number greater than two is the sum of two prime numbers. I have produced a designator which denotes that truth-value, but nobody (at the present date) knows whether the conjecture is true or false. It is not a sufficient condition for knowing what (or who) something is that one can produce a correct designation for the object. Suppose we retreat to a class of favored designations. Suppose I ask 'Who is the present mayor of Chicago?' and receive the answer, 'Richard J. Daley'. That would count as knowing who the mayor is on a T.V. quiz show. An answer 'true' or 'false' counts as knowing the truth-value of a sentence on a true-false examination. 'True' (or 'the true') is a favored name for the true as 'Richard J. Daley' is a favored name for the mayor.

One only has to consider another context to realize that being able to produce a favored name is not always a sufficient condition for knowing who (what). Suppose I am confronted with a police lineup and asked who among them is the mayor of Chicago. If I cannot pick him out of the lineup, can I be said to know who he is even if I say that he is 'Richard J. Daley'? What these examples illustrate is that sufficient conditions for knowing who (what) vary from one practical context to another and that no very useful general formula can be given concerning the matter. It is, of course, even more hopeless when it comes to necessary conditions. It is, however, much more difficult to think of circumstances in which being able to produce the standard name 'the true' would not be a sufficient condition for the producer to know the truth-value of the relevant sentence.

Granted this vagueness, we can still make clear enough sense of the idea that grasping the sense entails knowing the reference, albeit in a rather tenuous language-bound way. An attempt to make the connection less tenuous can be seen in the verifiability theory of the logical positivists. Their favored formula was that the meaning of a sentence is its method of verification. To know the meaning is to know the method of verification. Verification in the case of "empirical" propositions was taken to consist in having certain sensory experiences. Each sentence is thought of as associated with a set of sensory experiences such that having them constitutes the method of verifying that sentence. Since no sensory experience is relevant to the verification or falsification of a logical or an analytic truth, they come, on this theory, to be devoid of sense and so the positivists concluded. It is clear how far Frege was from any such verificationist view, but I hope that its elaboration throws some light on Frege's realist conception of sense. That conception is not correlated with a method of verification or proof, so that according to it there is no objection to the idea that one can understand a sentence (know the reference of a term) without having any idea whatever as to how to go about determining what the truth-value (referent) is.[22]

5

Negative Singular Existentials

I have presented the case for Russell's disguised description account of ordinary proper names as an argument that these two kinds of singular terms agree in their logical behavior. Kripke's modal arguments to the contrary were considered in the third chapter. John Searle and Wittgenstein also object to Russell's views. They say that the main difficulty with his theory is that it ignores a certain looseness in our use of proper names. Proper names, they say, are not, in general, associated by their users with unique descriptions as Russell's theory requires. Here Searle and Wittgenstein part company. Searle thinks that in place of the unique description required by Russell there are a cluster of descriptions which the users of a name associate with it. He thinks that it is a necessary truth that some "sufficiently large" (but indefinite) number of the open sentences on which these descriptions are built are uniquely satisfied by the referent of the name. Wittgenstein's correction to Russell's theory is rather different. He thinks proper names are characteristically used without any fixed meaning; there is neither a unique description nor a cluster of them which fixes the sense of our names. We use these names without a fixed sense.

Some looseness was already recognized by Frege. He says, "In the case of an actual proper name such as 'Aristotle' opinions as to the sense may differ. It might, for instance, be taken to be the following: the pupil of Plato and teacher of Alexander the Great. Anybody who does this will attach another sense to the sentence 'Aristotle was born in Stagira' than will a man who takes as the sense of the name: the teacher of Alexander the Great who was born in Stagira. So long as the reference remains the same, such variations of sense may be tolerated, although they are to be avoided in the theoretical structure of a demonstrative science and ought not to occur in a perfect language."[1] This is a different looseness than that discussed by either Searle or Wittgenstein; Frege's concerns different senses associated with the same name by different speakers, while the kind Searle and Wittgenstein deal with concerns a single speaker as well. It is, adding the views of the three authors, both interpersonal and intrapersonal. I find two difficulties in the quotation from Frege. He says, "So long as the reference remains the same, such variations may be tolerated . . ." What I suppose him to have been thinking is that though the propositions expressed by the sentence 'Aristotle was born in Stagira' are different for two people who attach different senses to 'Aristotle', still this difference is within tolerable limits because the propositions are not only both about Aristotle, they also have the same truth-value so long as the different senses associated with 'Aristotle' present the same referent. This is important if the two people are to communicate. But it all collapses as soon as we switch to consideration of sentences in indirect discourse, for example, 'John said that Aristotle was born in Stagira'. If, as in the general case, the speaker of this sentence attaches a different sense to 'Aristotle' than does the hearer, by Frege's principles the referent of that name in this sentence (namely, its customary sense) will also be different for these persons. Consequently, there is nothing to prevent the proposition expressed by the speaker of a sentence in indirect discourse from having a different truth-value from that of the proposition expressed by that same sentence for its hearer. So Frege's general assertion that, apart from a perfect language, such variation of sense "may be tolerated" cannot be accepted. Indeed, once we allow this much interpersonal looseness (or variation) in the senses attached to ordinary proper names, communication with sentences in indirect discourse becomes a quite mysterious affair. This is the first of the difficulties which I alluded to above as arising when it is allowed that various users of a name may associate different senses with it. Since it leads us into the general area of *oratio obliqua* constructions, we will set it aside for the present and turn to a second more immediately relevant difficulty.

What is unbelievable about Frege's account (and Russell is to be associated with him in this) is the contention that even though different persons may attach different senses to the same name, still any single individual attaches a unique sense to each name on all occasions (or even on any one occasion) of its use. At any rate, I can report as a mere matter of introspection that when I use 'Aristotle' I do not, in general, have any one description in mind which has the sense of that name for me. Not only do I not have any single description actually before my mind at the time of use of that name, I could not subsequently produce any description which would convey the sense which I attached to the name on any given occasion of its use, even granted that this description was not actually present to my mind on that occasion. That is, I could not in general; in some cases I can. In the case of some names of famous historical figures such as Homer, something like Russell's theory seems true. About all I know of Homer is that he is the author of the *Iliad* and the *Odyssey*. If asked to present a description which expressed the sense of that name, the only one I could come up with is 'the author of the *Iliad* and the *Odyssey*'. Concerning Thales, the description 'the Eleatic philosopher who believed that all is water' exhausts my information. But if we turn to people like my children, about whom I know an indefinitely large number of facts, Russell's theory seems a typical product of the philosopher's occupational disease, oversimplification. There is just not any one description which I can supply as expressing the sense of my wife's name because though I can produce an indefinitely large number of definite descriptions which denote her, no one of these stands out as having the privileged role of expressing the sense of her name. Perhaps such considerations led Russell to distinguish between those (such as our wives and children) whom we know "by acquaintance" and those (such as famous historical figures) whom we know only "by description." For Russell we possess names which are logically proper only for those objects known

95

to us by acquaintance. The names of those known only by description are really disguised descriptions.

The relevant classes do not really overlap so neatly. Among those I know "by description" are figures like Bertrand Russell and Ludwig Wittgenstein who are, in the relevant respect, like some of those I know by acquaintance. There is no unique definite description which I am prepared to acknowledge as substitutable for the names 'Bertrand Russell' or 'Ludwig Wittgenstein' on all or even one occasion of their use. The significant difference for our considerations is not that between knowledge by acquaintance and knowledge by description, but that between those of whom we know a great deal, whether acquaintances or not, and those such as Homer of whom we know hardly anything. It is only for these last cases that Russell's theory seems to have a chance of being adequate. The author of the article "Homer" in the *Encyclopaedia Britannica* (1959) seems to support this. He says, "The special difficulty about Homer is that, whereas David and Moses have an independent existence, whether or not they wrote the works ascribed to them, Homer has not: he is nothing but the author of the Homeric Poems. The poems are facts and 'Homer' a hypothesis to account for them." What the author means, I assume, is that 'Homer' is just short for 'the author of the Homeric Poems' so that it names whoever wrote these works, if indeed some unique individual did. Our author's view is that in every possible world 'Homer' denotes the same person as is denoted by 'the author of the Homeric Poems' in that world. The denotation of 'Homer' changes from one possible world to the next. There is even, I suppose, a possible world in which Homer is Plato, though there is no possible world in which Plato is not Plato. This, I think, is the point of a joke I recently heard. "You know, they have discovered that the *Iliad* and the *Odyssey* were not written by Homer but by another Greek with the same name." The point is that in any possible world, 'the author of the *Iliad* and the *Odyssey*' denotes Homer, if anything at all. Hence it could not have been discovered that these works were not written by him but by another man with the same name.

For these reasons 'Homer' seemed to be as good as we could do by way of a candidate for a name to which we attach some unique sense (or which abbreviates some unique definite description). But even about this name there are differences of opinion of the kind mentioned in the above quotation from Frege. The author of the article on Homer in the *Columbia Encyclopedia* (2d ed.) writes, "Modern scholars are generally agreed that there was a poet named Homer who lived before 700 B.C., probably in Asia Minor, that he wrote for an aristocratic society, and that the *Iliad* and the *Odyssey* are each the product of one poet's work, developed out of older legendary matter. Some assign the *Odyssey* to a poet who lived slightly after the author of the *Iliad*." Notice that this author assumes that if the *Iliad* and the *Odyssey* are the product of a single poet's work then they are the work of Homer. But he also considers the possibility that these works were written by different authors. In that case, is Homer the author of the *Iliad* or is he the author of the *Odyssey*? Or could he be neither the one nor the other though a real person nevertheless? I do not believe that clear answers to these questions are to be found among the authors on the vexed "Homeric question."

Those who recognize these difficulties but who do not want to abandon Russell's theory in spite of them are likely to respond that the theory can be made to work with only some minor adjustment to accommodate the looseness we have described. "Granted," these people say, "we cannot substitute any particular description which will do in place of a name on all occasions (or even on any single occasion) of its use, still we can supply a disjunction or cluster of such descriptions." Here is a brief statement of John Searle's modified Russellian view: "Suppose we ask the users of the name 'Aristotle' to state what they regard as certain essential and established facts about him. Their answers would be a set of uniquely referring descriptive statements. Now what I am arguing is that the descriptive force of 'This is Aristotle' is to assert that a sufficient but so far unspecified number of these statements are true of this subject."[2]

Another statement of a similar view is that contained in the passage on Moses in Wittgenstein's *Philosophical Investigations*,[3] quoted in the last chapter.

Here, then, are views of Searle and Wittgenstein which are modifications of Russell's theory. According to Searle, ordinary proper names mean the same as some disjunction of a number (or more vaguely defined "cluster") of descriptions—in any case, not just one. These views further emphasize that the descriptions which are associated with a name can shift from speaker to speaker and from occasion to occasion. What is at stake, according to Searle, when we speculate concerning whether or not there was a historical Moses—whether or not Moses ever existed —is not whether some one definite description has a unique denotation (as with Russell) but whether a "sufficient but so far unspecified number" of a rather loosely defined set or disjunction of descriptions have a unique denotation. There is an interesting difference in the two quotations. Searle simply asks what the users of a name would *say* if *asked* certain questions. Wittgenstein, in the first part of my quotation from him, considers the meanings which 'Moses did not exist' may have—a rather different question. We have all along been following Searle's method, that is, considering the crucial question to be what people would say by way of producing descriptions associated with a given name. It is not at all clear that this is what is at stake in the issue as to what, if any, sense is attached to a name. But it is commonly enough assumed that this is what is at issue, as in the quotation from Searle and in the last part of the quotation from Wittgenstein where he goes on to consider the things we might say we mean by 'Moses'. Wittgenstein thus indicates that he regards the two questions as amounting to the same thing.

The classical theory, especially as modified by Searle and Wittgenstein, has a great deal to recommend it. These views provide answers to some philosophical questions about proper names. Searle does not regard his theory as involving a mere minor correction of Russell's. He thinks that his theory avoids further mistakes which Russell makes. We will turn to these considerations shortly, but before doing so I would like to consider further the view expressed by Wittgenstein.

Wittgenstein's idea is that we do not use a name such as 'Moses' with a fixed meaning, so that if the question arises 'Is there a historical Moses? Did he really exist?', there is nothing definite at issue in advance. That is, we can ask 'Did Moses exist?' without having fixed in advance what we would have to know in order to conclude that he did or did not exist. It is not settled by our ordinary use of the name 'Moses', whether if it were discovered that he never led the Israelites out of Egypt we would have to conclude that he did not exist at all. What would we have to discover to justify this conclusion? According to Wittgenstein this is not settled. At least not in general, for in some cases where our information is extremely meager, with such a name, for example, as 'St. Anne', it is settled. If the mother of Mary did not exist, St. Anne did not exist. But this is a special case because all the information I have about St. Anne is that she was the mother of Mary. It would simply be impossible for me to understand the claim that though the mother of Mary did not exist, St. Anne was a real historical person.

According to Wittgenstein, I am prepared to find any number of my beliefs about Moses mistaken, but after a certain point I would conclude that my mistake was not that I believed him to have performed certain deeds he did not do, but that he never existed at all. Only it is not fixed in advance where that point is. It is clear that this view is not the cluster theory discussed by Kripke in "Naming and Necessity," and refuted by him. Kripke says, "there is a popular modern substitute for the theory of Frege and Russell. . . . The substitute is that, although a name is not a disguised description it either abbreviates, or anyway its reference is determined by some cluster of descriptions. The question is whether this is true . . . There are stronger and weaker versions of this. The stronger version would say that the name is simply defined, synonymously, as the cluster of descriptions. It will then be necessary not that Moses had any particular property in this cluster, but that he had the disjunction of them."[4] It makes no difference to the logical point at issue whether we take the single property or the cluster of properties view. So for simplicity, let us just consider the single property view.

It is a principal aim of Russell's theory to provide an account of the logical form of negative existential assertions such as 'Moses did not exist'. The question whether Moses exists, according to Russell, means the same as 'Was there a single person who led the Israelites out of Egypt?', if the unique description for which 'Moses' is the surrogate for the speaker is 'the man who led the Israelites out of Egypt'. I have already said that, in general, it is false that we do have any such unique description in mind. But suppose we overlook this false empirical claim. Suppose it true, as Russell's theory claims, that there always is such a unique description present. Or, consider the modification of the classical theory advocated by Searle according to which the speaker has in mind some cluster of descriptions which supply the sense of a proper name on any occasion of its use. Is it true that the question 'Did Moses exist?' means what these theories say it does? I think that we can easily convince ourselves that these theories are wrong. Suppose that no single man acted as leader to take the Israelites out of Egypt and indeed that a great many, if not most, of our other commonly held beliefs about Moses are false. We can still suppose that, nevertheless, he was a real person who played an extremely important role in the early history of the Hebrew people. Even if we are wrong in many, or even most, of our commonly held beliefs about Moses and discover that we are, we need not conclude (though we may) that Moses did not exist. The theory is all the more implausible in the simple version advanced by Russell according to which there is always some unique definite description associated with the name of a historical figure such that if it were discovered that the open sentence in the description was not uniquely satisfied, we would have to conclude that the historical figure in question did not exist. The trouble with Russell's view is that according to it such a discovery is known by us *a priori* to be impossible. And the same is true for the modified view of Searle. They make it a matter of *a priori* truth that our main beliefs about historical figures cannot be false. But surely they can. The trouble with all of these views is that they are infected with psychologism. According to them, whether or not a person exists cannot be separated from the question of the truth or falsity of our beliefs about that person, and this is wrong. Most of my central beliefs about a real historical figure might be false of him.

Russell's theory is wrong for another reason. All or most of my beliefs about Moses might be true of another person. Someone else (not Moses) might have led the Jews out of Egypt and received the ten commandments on Sinai. The trouble with Russell's theory is that it entails that this is not possible. It entails that if any single person did the deeds commonly attributed to Moses, it must have been Moses. Let us be clear exactly where the error lies. A defender of Russell might reply as follows: "Look, for me 'Moses' is just short for 'the man who led the Israelites out of Egypt', that is all the name means to me, so it just does not make sense for me to suppose that someone other than Moses did that. That would be to suppose that the man who led the Israelites out of Egypt did not lead the Israelites out of Egypt and that is only possible if Moses did not exist. So I cannot suppose that Moses *exists* and that he did not lead the Israelites out of Egypt." There is, of course, no logical fallacy here. It all follows once it is assumed that 'Moses' is just short for 'the man who led the Israelites out of Egypt'. But if this is the case for 'Moses' for a particular person, it is certainly not the case for that name for most of the people who use it and it is not the case for most names. Most of us can suppose that though Moses existed, we are wrong in attributing that deed to him because someone else led the Israelites out of Egypt. For most of us, the question of whether Moses existed is not the question of whether anyone did most of the deeds we believe him to have done or some special subset of them. But that is the contention of those who accept the disguised description theory of Russell, and the modification sometimes called the "cluster theory" of Searle.

We can deny Russell's theory about ordinary proper names while continuing to recognize that it is an interesting question whether or not anyone ever did all or any of the things that

Socrates, or Moses, or Homer, is said to have done, or whether anyone ever did a "sufficiently large" number of these things. The point is that even if we have affirmative answers to these questions, even if we have conclusive evidence that someone did indeed do all or some of these things, it is another question, not yet decided, whether that person (whoever he was) was Socrates, or Homer, or Moses. The classical theory about 'Did Socrates exist?' and its recent loosening seem plausible only because these two questions are not kept separated. Perhaps ordinary usage is not precise at this point either. If the question is raised 'Did Socrates exist?', perhaps it is not entirely clear whether the questioner wants to know whether anyone ever actually did any one or a "sufficiently large" number of the things that Socrates is said to have done, not caring whether that person was Socrates or not, or whether the questioner wants to know whether we, and those who introduced the name to us, are referring to a real person, namely, Socrates. But if this unclarity exists in ordinary usage, it can also be removed. The trouble with the Russell-Searle views is that they rest on a confusion of the two questions.

Searle says, "I am suggesting it is a necessary fact that Aristotle has the logical sum, inclusive disjunction of properties commonly attributed to him: any individual not having at least some of these properties could not be Aristotle."[5] After quoting the passage about Moses from Wittgenstein, Kripke says "The gist of all this is that we know *a priori* that if the Biblical story is substantially false, Moses did not exist. I have already argued that the Biblical story does not give *necessary* properties of Moses, that he might have lived without doing any of these things. Here I ask whether we know *a priori* that if Moses existed he in fact did some or most of them."[6] I have argued, in the third chapter, that it does not follow from Russell's theory that if 'Aristotle' is replaced by 'the teacher of Alexander' then it is a necessary truth that Aristotle is a teacher. The proposition 'Necessarily the teacher of Alexander is a teacher' is true *de dicto* but false *de re*. But in any case Kripke is right to object to any theory which maintains that it is a necessary truth that Aristotle or Moses possesses all or most of the properties commonly attributed to him. I agree with Kripke that we do not know *a priori* that if Moses existed he did all or most of the things commonly attributed to him. And if Kripke is right about this, then the classical theory of Russell and its modification by Searle are both mistaken. But Kripke's argument on this point is conclusive. Referring to Wittgenstein's treatment of 'Moses' he says,

> The Biblical story might have been a complete legend, *or it might have been a substantially false account of a real person.* In the latter case, it seems to me that a scholar could say that he supposes that, though Moses did exist, the things said of him in the Bible are substantially false. . . . Suppose someone says that no prophet ever was swallowed by a big fish or whale. Does it follow, on that basis, that Jonah did not exist? There still seems to be the question whether the Biblical account is a legendary account of no person or a legendary account built on a real person. In the latter case, it's only natural to say that, though Jonah did exist, no one did the things commonly related to him. I choose this case because while Biblical scholars generally hold that Jonah did exist, the account not only of his being swallowed by a big fish but even going to Nineveh to preach or anything else that is said in the Biblical story is assumed to be sub-stantially false.[7]

A principal advantage of Russell's theory of ordinary proper names is that it offers a solution to the problem of negative existential propositions. It provides an answer to the question 'What is at issue when we consider the question of the historical reality of Moses, Jesus, Homer, and so on?' We have given reasons for rejecting this account. What we found wrong in the classical theory is its psychologism; it makes the existence of, for example, Moses depend upon whether or not our commonly held beliefs about him are true. Put this way it is evident, of course, that the view is wrong for this statement of the view is itself incoherent. The incoherence takes this form. According to this view, if most of our commonly held beliefs about Moses are mistaken, then Moses did not exist. But if these beliefs *are about Moses,* he did exist. One wants to protest: "Surely whether

Moses existed or not has nothing whatever to do with our beliefs about him or what we know. Indeed it has nothing whatever to do with us at all." But that is not quite true, for a connection can be made. The question of whether Moses existed or not can have an affirmative answer only if our commonly held beliefs about Moses are beliefs about a real person, whether or not these commonly held beliefs are true or false. This is a very different matter from these beliefs being true of a real person, for they well might be true of a real person other than Moses.

Our conclusion is that most of the things we commonly believe about Moses or Aristotle could be false. But could all of these beliefs be false? Notice that in the last quoted passage from Kripke he considers two possibilities, the Biblical account may be a legendary account of no person, or a legendary account of a real person. Might it also be a legendary account of a real nonperson, a dog? Could Aristotle be a citizen of Berlin born in 1933? Among the things we commonly believe about Aristotle are that he was a person and that he was born in antiquity. It seems that we could not be wrong about these things. Aristotle and Moses were both essentially human. Of course they might not have existed at all, but given that they existed they were necessarily persons. So our conclusion is that though most of the things we believe about Aristotle and Moses might be false, still not all of them can be. This admission does not lead to rehabilitation of Russell's theory, for being born in antiquity and being a person are hardly properties upon which to build a definite description uniquely denoting Aristotle; and it must be admitted that Searle is right when he says that "it is a necessary fact that Aristotle has the logical sum, inclusive disjunction, of properties commonly attributed to him," for it is a necessary fact that Aristotle was human, and that is one of the properties commonly attributed to him.

None of these observations, however, work against the view of Wittgenstein. Indeed, it seems that just such a view is needed to account for them. Wittgenstein's view is that we do not ordinarily use proper names with a "fixed meaning." What I have taken this to mean is that generally when we use names of historical figures there need be nothing definite at issue in the question 'Was there a historical Moses (Homer, Napoleon)?'. By that I mean that it need not be fixed in advance what facts, if discovered, would lead us to conclude that some, or all, of these people never existed. But we do sometimes decide this, and sometimes the question is left undecided, open. I can imagine easily that future scholars might conclude that only one of the two works usually ascribed to him was actually written by Homer, perhaps the *Iliad*, perhaps the *Odyssey*. But it seems quite certain that a discovery that neither of these works was written by any single person would be the discovery that Homer was not a real historical person. In the case of most names, however, Wittgenstein is surely right. We cannot now say precisely what would have to be shown to establish that there was no historical Moses.

Does this mean the total abandonment of Russell's analysis of negative existentials? I think not. It does mean that we must supplement Russell's account with something like Wittgenstein's. Russell's account of the logic of negative singular existentials should be regarded as giving their analysis after our language (or the relevant portion of it) has been regimented so as to eliminate the vagueness (and ambiguity) which infects its normal use. For some purposes this vagueness becomes intolerable. It may be necessary for certain purposes to fix the meaning of a name which ordinarily is used without a fixed meaning. One such purpose may be that of deciding the issue of the historical reality of a Moses or Homer. When this is done, when the sense of the name is fixed, the logical form of a negative singular existential assertion will be exactly what Russell said it was.

Kripke's theory of names as rigid designators is associated with another theory sometimes called "the causal theory" or "the historical theory" of names. Versions of the causal theory have been advocated by several authors and the theory gives rise to alternative solutions to some of the problems that the description theory was designed to solve. These accounts stress the history which leads up to our present use of a name. Donnellan gives this version:

In general, our use of proper names for persons in history (and also those we are not personally acquainted with) is parasitic on uses of the names by other people—in conversation, written records, etc. Insofar as we possess a set of identifying descriptions in these cases they come from things said about the presumed referent by other people. My answer to the question, 'Who was Thales?' would probably derive from what I learned from my teachers or from histories of philosophy. Frequently, as in this example, one's identifying descriptions trace back through many levels of parasitic derivation. Descriptions of Thales we might give go back to what was said, using that name, by Aristotle and Herodotus. And if Thales existed, the trail would not end there.[8]

The picture which emerges is that of a name being bestowed on a person (perhaps in a baptismal ceremony) and then being handed down to others, perhaps through many generations. One person introduces it to others and fixes its reference with a backing of descriptions; the name is handed down from link to link until it finally gets introduced to us. The question of whether the name, for example, 'Socrates', has a referent concerns the structure of this causal chain. Does it begin with an actual person, perhaps in a ceremony in which the name is bestowed, or is there no tracing the use of the name back through the chain of causation to an actual person at all?

We can now see what there is to "the cluster of descriptions" theory of names. The definite descriptions associated with a name serve to fix the referent of the name in the historical chain through which it is transmitted from link to link down to us. But it would be a mistake to conclude from this that the name, say 'Socrates', necessarily denotes the same as any one of these descriptions (Russell) or the same as some "sufficiently large" disjunction of them (Searle). Consider the descriptions we might employ to introduce the name 'Socrates' to a group of students: 'the teacher of Plato', 'the husband of Xantippe', 'the philosopher who died by drinking the hemlock in 399 B.C.', and so on. Suppose, as with Russell's view, that 'Socrates' is a "truncated" form of 'the teacher of Plato'. It would follow that we could not discover that the real Socrates was not Plato's teacher. But surely we could discover this. Surely it is conceivable that that part of the historical account is false, a fabrication. But the same is true of any other single description we can form except for such question-begging ones as 'the person identical with Socrates'. Surely we could discover that Socrates was not really the husband of Xantippe, not really the teacher of Plato, not really put to death by the Athenian people. All of these stories could have been fabricated about a real person, Socrates.

Kripke says, "I want to present just a *better picture* than the picture presented by the received views."[9] He does not claim that the causal theory presents a set of necessary and sufficient conditions for reference. He even gives an example against its sufficiency. "There may be a causal chain from our use of the term 'Santa Claus' to a certain historical saint, but still the children, when they use this, by this time probably do not refer to that saint. So other conditions must be satisfied in order to make this into a really rigorous theory of reference."[10] To dwell a bit on the example, suppose my use of 'Santa Claus' can be traced back from link to link to an actual person about whom the legend gradually grew. We cannot conclude from this that I am referring to that person in my use of the name. At this point we can say with certainty that Santa Claus is a legendary figure and it does not matter at all whether our use of the name can in fact be traced back to a real person. At some point the legendary Santa Claus got detached from the real person, and we are referring to the legendary figure not the real one. So we can also say, quite certainly, that Santa Claus does not exist. We cannot be refuted by tracing our use of the name back to a real person, for we are not referring to that person but to the legendary figure. We see, then, that the causal theory does not provide an analysis of singular negative existentials. We might think that it does and suppose the account to go somewhat like this: 'Santa Claus does not exist' is true if and only if our use of 'Santa Claus' cannot be traced back in the causal chain to a real person. We see that even if it can be traced to a real person it does not follow that Santa

Claus exists because we are not referring to that person, but to a legendary figure when we use 'Santa Claus'. The general principle is that what matters is who or what we *now* are referring to when we use a name, not who or what those who introduced the name, perhaps thousands of years ago, were referring to. We are not communicating with people who lived that long ago and have no responsibility to make our use of language conform with theirs. We are communicating with our contemporaries and it is to their use of language which we are required to conform on pain of not being understood.

What has happened in this particular case is that in the process of transmitting the name 'Santa Claus' the intention to refer to the real person was at some point abandoned in favor of the intention to refer to the legendary figure. If I am to be referring to N.N. in my use of the name 'N.N.', what is sufficient is that my use of this name can be traced back in a causal chain to N.N. where at each point that the name is handed on the intention to maintain the reference of the giver of the name is retained by the receiver. The name is passed from link to link preserving the intention to refer to the same object as is referred to by the person(s) who give us the name. With this clause added, the causal theory does indeed provide a sufficient condition for a name, in a given use, to refer to a certain object. It does not provide an analysis of reference since it presupposes this notion. Without appeal to the intention to preserve reference, the theory does not supply a sufficient condition for a use of a name, on a given occasion, to refer to a given object. Kripke acknowledges this. "When the name is 'passed from link to link', the receiver of the name must, I think, intend when he learns it to use it with the same reference as the man from whom he heard it. If I hear the name 'Napoleon' and decide it would be a nice name for my pet aardvark, I do not satisfy the condition. (Perhaps it is some such failure to keep the reference fixed which accounts for the divergence of the present uses of 'Santa Claus' from the alleged original use.)"[11] He adds, "Notice that the preceding outline hardly *eliminates* the notion of reference; on the contrary, it takes the notion of intending to use the same reference as a given."[12]

Does the theory nevertheless provide a necessary condition for reference? If I say "Aristotle said that all men by nature desire to know," is it a necessary condition for me to be referring to Aristotle that my use of this name be traceable back to him? It does not seem to me to be so. Suppose, in fact, that my use of 'Aristotle' can be traced back to an illiterate Athenian who never said anything so profound as that all men by nature desire to know. Suppose that through some mistake or conscious fraud the works we attribute to the philosopher have been attributed to Aristotle. Is it clear that we would be wrong to say, "Aristotle said that all men by nature desire to know"? I think not. I think that by now it does not matter about the fraud. It is not a necessary condition for me to be referring to Aristotle that my use of his name can be traced back in the causal chain to him. When I say "Aristotle said that all men by nature desire to know," I am referring to the author of the work known to us as "Aristotle's *Metaphysics*," whoever that may be.

We must not, however, overlook the very tentative character of the claims which are made with regard to the causal theory of names. The necessary condition thesis can be understood as a very weak claim which says merely that though we may refer to things in no way causally connected with us with descriptions, we cannot do so with names. In the case just discussed, the historical chain leads back to several individuals, one of which is the actual author of the *Metaphysics*, whoever he is. Kripke, at any rate, does not claim to supply either a necessary or a sufficient condition for reference. "I want to present a better picture without giving a set of necessary and sufficient conditions for reference. Such conditions would be very complicated, but what is true is that it's in virtue of our connection with other speakers in the community, going back to the referent himself, that we refer to a certain man."[13]

Suppose we grant the necessary condition thesis of the causal theory understood as this very weak claim. A question remains concerning the role the causal theory plays in a theory of meaning or reference for our language. What is it a theory about? It cannot be taken to be part of an account of the sense of sentences containing proper names, part of an account of what we understand when we understand these sentences, or what we claim to know when we know them to be true. If I claim to know that Socrates drank the hemlock in 399 B.C., it is surely utterly unrealistic to maintain that I am claiming to know anything whatever about the chain of acquisition which brings the name 'Socrates' down to me across the centuries, for I have no such knowledge and claim none. Nevertheless, I claim to know that Socrates did drink the hemlock in 399 B.C. What I claim to know involves the sense of the name 'Socrates', and that I must grasp if I am to understand any sentence containing that name. The causal theory of names is not part of a theory of sense. What then is its office? It is hardly open to objection if all that is claimed is that I acquire names from others who in turn acquire them from others back to some point of origin. The same is true of all words. This explains nothing about what any word means. The causal theorists seem to claim that the theory provides an account of truth-conditions for sentences involving names. This has the consequence that the verification of such sentences involves the tracing of chains of causation which no one knows anything about. It makes it utterly obscure how we can know anything about Socrates or Plato at all.[14]

Conclusion

Russell's theory, according to which an ordinary proper name is "short for" a unique definite description, is wrong. 'Does Aristotle exist?' does not mean 'Does the teacher of Alexander exist?', nor does it mean the same as this question with any other single description, of the kind Russell gives as examples, in place of 'the teacher of Alexander'. Searle's cluster theory is also wrong for similar reasons. The question of whether Aristotle existed is not the same as the question of whether some "sufficiently large" number of our beliefs about Aristotle are true. We can take any disjunction of our commonly held beliefs about Aristotle and find that most of them are false of him. But Wittgenstein's modification of Russell is different from Searle's. It is a genuine alternative to both Searle and Russell as well as to Kripke's causal theory. The question of the historical reality of a figure of antiquity is never investigated by an attempt to trace the causal chain of acquisition back "from link to link" through thousands of years. That is clearly impossible. What we in fact do, is to investigate the truth of our commonly held beliefs. If enough of the centrally important of these prove false, we will conclude that the supposed historical personage never existed. It is not that we can say in advance of any historical investigation which of our beliefs must be sustained, so that the question 'Did Aristotle exist?' has an exact meaning involving some fixed cluster. That is Searle's view. What is true is that if enough of the ground is cut from beneath us we will give up the name. But we cannot say now exactly what that ground is. It becomes fixed as we go along. Or else it does not and we do not know what to conclude from our investigation.

The way to look at Russell's theory is as a regimented model or formal counterpart of a portion of natural language. Ordinary language contains vague and ambiguous terms and there is no precise logic which they obey. For certain purposes this vagueness and ambiguity is a useful and desirable trait of our language, as Wittgenstein has pointed out with great force. For certain other purposes, the purposes of exact reasoning, this vagueness and ambiguity become intolerable and must be eliminated. The elimination need not be effected for all time, but only for purposes of a current discussion. In this way the questions 'Did Homer exist?', 'Did Moses exist?' are vague. We can remove this vagueness, if necessary, in a given context. When we do, we will fix on a definite description or "cluster"of them for which we will take these names as "abbreviations," as Russell says. The logical form of 'Homer does not exist' and of the other singular positive, or negative, existentials is then what Russell says it is.

II

Reference and Modality

6

Quine's Attack on Modal Logic

I

Singular terms and the sign of identity are intimately connected by logic and syntax. They require this sign to be flanked by these terms in well-formed sentences. This intimate connection has been emphasized by W. V. Quine, who has explicated its logical significance in his *principle of substitutivity. The terms of a true statement of identity are everywhere intersubstitutive, salva veritate.*[1] Given the truth of 'Socrates is the teacher of Plato' and 'The teacher of Plato is the husband of Xantippe', the principle yields the truth of 'Socrates is the husband of Xantippe'. This is different from the principle formulated in *Principia Mathematica*[2] which identifies identity with indiscernibility as follows:

$$(1) \quad (x = y) = \text{df. } (\varphi)(\varphi x \equiv \varphi y).$$

Wittgenstein, in the *Tractatus,* objects to this identification. The objection is that "Russell's definition of '=' is inadequate, because according to it we cannot say that two objects have all their properties in common. (Even if this proposition is never correct, it still has sense)."[3] Statement (1) says not only that if x and y are identical they share all their properties; it provides for the converse as well: that objects cannot, in Leibniz's phrase, differ *solo numero.* Wittgenstein's objection is to this implication of Russell's definition. The idea of objects differing only numerically has been introduced solely that it may be set aside. It is not at issue in the *principle of the indiscernibility of identicals,* which states that identical objects have the same properties (do not differ qualitatively). One may or may not agree with Wittgenstein that qualitative identity does not entail numerical identity, but one cannot coherently think that numerical identity does not entail the qualitative sort.

The principle of substitutivity appears to be merely a formal-mode version of the indiscernibility of identicals, but it lacks the self-evidence of the latter; its justification, however, is easily found in classical semantical considerations. Logic teaches us to analyze statements as arising from open sentences by binding of their free variables or by replacement of these by singular terms. Open sentences are expressions that are true of certain objects and false of others. For example, a true statement results from the open sentence '*x* is a Greek' when some name, or other singular designation, for some object of which the open sentence is true replaces the variable '*x*'.

Given this semantical analysis, together with some further details, we see why the principle of substitutivity has been accepted; for that the terms of a true identity-statement are everywhere intersubstitutive, *salva veritate,* is merely explicative of the idea of singular terms having singular reference. The reasoning is as follows. By replacing, with an appropriate variable, any singular term in one or more of its occurrences in each statement containing at least one singular term, we construct a class of (one-place) open sentences. Any singular term thus replaced in a true statement refers to an object that satisfies the open sentence thus constructed. An object satisfies such an open sentence only if replacing the open sentence's free variable by *any* singular term making reference to the object turns the open sentence into a true statement. (The converse of this conditional is not correct because it is not assumed that every object in the range of our variables is designated by some singular term. The conditional itself holds for all objects in the range of our variables, albeit vacuously of those without designations.) Consequently, the result of replacing a singular term in a true statement by any other singular term referring to the same object leaves the truth-value of the host statement unchanged. Terms of a true identity-statement refer to the same thing. And with this we have a proof of the principle of substitutivity.

II

The principle of substitutivity is explicative of the concept of singular reference, so it is of the idea of quantification. The statement $(\exists x)F(x)$ is true if and only if there is at least one object in the range of the variable that satisfies the open sentence $F(x)$. If it be granted that $F(a)$ is true (where 'a' is a singular term), and that it remains true under substitution of coreferential terms for 'a', then, by the semantical account already given, we have our satisfying object in a. Consequently, $(\exists x)F(x)$ is also true. The inference by existential generalization is justified because in performing it we are merely abstracting from the particular mode of designating an object in a true statement where no particular mode of designation is relevant to the truth of that statement. Failure of the inference from $F(a)$ to $(\exists x)F(x)$ occurs if and only if 'a' fails of singular reference in $F(a)$. For example, the inference from 'Pegasus does not exist' to $(\exists x)$ (x does not exist) fails because nothing satisfies the open sentence 'x does not exist'. Failure of substitutivity for a term in a given context entails failure of reference for that term in that context. For this reason, by the present argument, it entails failure of existential generalization on that term as well. Contexts productive of failure of substitutivity are for this reason called by Quine "referentially opaque." Our argument shows that we cannot sensibly quantify into referentially opaque contexts.

III

The principle of substitutivity has now come to be seen as an integral part of the semantics of classical quantification theory. On the other hand, hardly is the principle stated before one finds cases contrary to it. The true identity 'Cicero = Tully' will not support the substitution of 'Cicero' for 'Tully' in ' 'Tully' consists

117

of five letters'. This is not a genuine paradox, for *substitutivity* is wrongly applied to terms in contexts in which they do not refer "simply" to their denotations. ' 'Tully' consists of five letters' is not about Cicero (= Tully) but about one of his names. According to Quine, lapse of substitutivity merely reveals that the occurrence of the name supplanted is not "purely referential" because "the statement depends not only on the subject, but on the form of the name."[4] Quotation is only the most blatant of contexts in which terms can fail of purely referential occurrence. Consider, 'Philip believes that Tegucigalpa is in Nicaragua'. Misuse of substitutivity will take us from this and 'Tegucigalpa = the capital of Honduras' to the falsehood 'Philip believes that the capital of Honduras is in Nicaragua'. Here again, for Quine, failure of substitutivity is only symptomatic of 'Tegucigalpa's' failure of purely referential occurrence at the place of substitution. "The contexts 'is unaware that . . .' and 'believes that . . .' *resemble* the context of single quotes in this respect: a name may occur referentially in a statement S and not occur referentially in a longer statement which is formed by embedding S in the context 'is unaware that . . .' or 'believes that . . .' "[5] For Quine, these contexts are all referentially opaque, and logical necessity provides but another example. It is a true contingent statement that

(2) 9 = the number of the planets.

It is further true that

(3) $\Box(9>7)$.

But replacement of '9' in (3) by 'the number of the planets' by virtue of (2) yields

(4) $\Box(\text{the number of the planets} >7)$,

which is false.

Quine's concepts of the referentially opaque context and the purely referential occurrence of singular terms reflect the standpoint of the semantics of classical predicate logic. From that standpoint, the principle of substitutivity is analytic of the idea of singular reference, and we are left with no alternative but to conclude that '9' in □(9>7) does not make singular reference to 9. We cannot, in our semantics, make the view coherent that '9' refers to the object 9 in (3), in view of the truth of (2) and (3) and the falsity of (4). Quine does leave us to suppose that terms which fail to refer "simply" to their objects (or which fail of "purely" referential occurrence), in some unexplained fashion still manage to refer, only not purely or simply. But this part of his theory is never developed.

Referential opacity poses a problem because our semantics is inapplicable to opaque contexts. On analysis, □(9>7) does not yield an open sentence □(*x*>7) from which it results by replacement of '*x*' *by* '9'. The sentence □(*x*>7) cannot, coherently, be taken as an open sentence, for given an open sentence and an object within the range of its variable, either the open sentence is true or it is false of that object. Is our purported open sentence true of the object 9? Since the number of planets *is* 9, an affirmative answer is incompatible with the falsity of (4), and a negative answer is incompatible with the truth of (3). Thus, □(*x*>7) is not an open sentence at all. But if the numeral '9' does not name an object in □(9>7) which satisfies the open sentence □(*x*>7), what role is it performing there? How is its presence relevant to the truth of the sentence containing it? Our inability to answer this question reveals that we do not know the logical form of such statements.

We have above explored the intimate connection in classical semantics between singular terms and quantification. The inference by existential generalization from $F(a)$ to $(\exists x)F(x)$ is valid if and only if '*a*' makes singular reference in $F(a)$. We have had to abandon the view that '9' refers to 9, in (3). It is an easy step to conclude, and Quine does conclude, that

$$(5) \quad (\exists x)\Box(x>7)$$

is unintelligible; we cannot sensibly *quantify into* referentially opaque contexts. What (5) seems to say is that there is something such that it is necessarily greater than 7. But Quine asks, "What is this number which according to [5] is necessarily greater than 7? According to [3] from which [5] was inferred, it was 9, that

119

is, the number of planets; but to suppose this would conflict with the fact that [4] is false."[6] The difficulty arises because necessary or contingent traits of objects are taken to belong to them not absolutely but according to whether one way of specifying them is used rather than another. Nine is taken to be necessarily greater than seven according to whether it is specified as in (3) but not as in (4). Hence the difference in truth-value between (3) and (4) and the consequent obscurity of (5). The modal logician, saddled as he is with (5), is thus committed to a metaphysical view, "Aristotelian essentialism" to give it a name, according to which necessary and contingent properties do belong to objects irrespective of their modes of specification, if specified at all. It is a doctrine which is required to make sense of (5) in spite of the difference in truth-value of (3) and (4), and the truth of (2), that is, in spite of the classical semantics of quantification. "Evidently," says Quine, "this reversion to Aristotelian essentialism is required if quantification into modal contexts is to be insisted on." He concludes, "So much the worse for quantified modal logic."[7]

IV

We have assumed that if '9' names an object in (3), what it names is 9. By abandoning the assumption that in opaque contexts names stand for their ordinary references, Frege was able to provide an analysis that did not take these contexts as productive of reference failure.[8] From a Fregean point of view, such contexts are incorrectly characterized as "referentially opaque." For Frege, they are producers of reference shift rather than reference failure, and he calls them "oblique." The references of names in oblique contexts are what, in ordinary contexts, are their senses. For Frege, it is false that '9' in (2) and '9' in (3) have the same reference; there is a fallacy of ambiguity in passing from (2) and (3) to (4). So, for Frege, there is no such thing as referential opacity, where the criterion for this is failure of substitutivity. In (2), '9' has the same reference as 'the number of the planets' but a different sense. This sense is the (oblique) reference of '9' in (3).

In an early paper[9] Quine exploits a distinction between *meaning* and *designation* which is very like Frege's distinction between sense and reference. If we pursue the similarity and adopt, for Quine's pair of concepts, the Fregean principle that in oblique contexts the designations of names are their meanings, we have a proof at hand that there are no opaque contexts. On our Fregean assumption, the principle of substitutivity allows replacement of names in oblique contexts only by synonymous names; and reference now is taken as context-relative. Hence the principle of substitutivity is recast so as to affirm the replaceability of any term in a given context by any other term having the same reference as the first *in that context*. Since we cannot change the meaning of a statement, ordinary or oblique, by replacing any of its constituents by a synonym, such substitution cannot change truth-values. If, with Quine, we take failure of substitutivity as a criterion of referential opacity,[10] there are no longer any referentially opaque contexts. By shifting the domain of discourse, we retain our semantics, and the old analysis continues its applicability to the misnamed opaque contexts.

V

If we assume, with Frege, that the reference of a complex name is a function of the references of its constituent names and that the reference of a (declarative) sentence is its truth-value, we have a proof that $\Box(9>7)$ remains true under every replacement of '9' by a name having the same ordinary sense as '9', provided that '9' is assumed to name that sense in that sentence. Under this last assumption, $\Box(x>7)$ may be treated as an open sentence true of this sense. Failure of substitutivity in oblique contexts reveals that the relevant names differ in their ordinary senses. To defend his thesis that numbers are objects, Frege thought it necessary to provide a sense for statements of identity between numbers, and between numbers and other objects.[11] If, now, we take senses to be objects, we must also provide them with identity-conditions. It is somewhat surprising that Frege himself made no attempt to do this. Lacking an independent identity-condition for senses, the principle that coreferential terms are everywhere intersubstitutive tells us only that names may replace each other, *salva veritate,* wherever they can. Senses as *objects* become idle wheels turning nothing. In Quine's phrase, "No entity without identity."[12]

But, far from paving the way for the happy marriage of quantification and modality, Frege's theory of reference makes the union inevitably barren. On Frege's view, what can we make of statements in which names appear both inside and outside the scope of opacity-inducing operators? Consider

(6)   9 is greater than 7, and necessarily 9 is greater than 7.

According to Frege, the object here said to be greater than 7 is not the same as the object said to be necessarily greater than 7. But this is not what is intended in (6); (6) is intended as synonymous with

(7)   9 is greater than 7, and necessarily it is greater than 7.

The difficulty is that, for Frege, (7) must be sheer nonsense because the pronoun 'it' inside the scope of the modal operator cannot pick up the reference of the numeral '9' outside the scope of that operator. If the pronoun did pick up the reference of the numeral, it would refer to the object 9 rather than a sense, and this Frege denies. Pronouns being the equivalents of bound variables in ordinary language, we see that Frege's theory is incapable of reflecting the interplay between occurrences of terms both inside and outside the scopes of modal operators that statements of modality are ordinarily taken to express. We have an argument against the intelligibility of quantification into oblique contexts.

VI

When Frege came to deal with oblique contexts, he decided that names in them referred to their ordinary senses and not their ordinary references. Suppose that identity-statements which are not merely true but necessarily true must contain terms whose ordinary senses are the same. Then given Frege's principle identifying oblique reference with ordinary sense, necessary identity-statements would sustain substitution in necessity contexts. If we now further suppose that all true identity-statements are necessarily true, all our purported examples of the referential opacity of necessity will be swept aside and safely accounted fallacies.

At one time, Quine thought that by intensionalizing the values of our variables in this way we would render all true identities necessarily true and so clear the way to quantified modal logic. In a letter to Rudolf Carnap published in *Meaning and Necessity,* Quine says, "I agree that such adherence to an intensional ontology, with extrusion of extensional entities altogether from the range of values of the variables, is indeed an effective way of reconciling quantification and modality. The cases of conflict between quantification and modality depend on extensions as values of variables. In your object language we may unhesitatingly quantify modalities because extensions have been dropped from among the values of the variables; even the individuals of the concrete world have disappeared, leaving only their concepts behind them."[13] The purging of concrete individuals from the universe of discourse, Quine thought, would leave us with intensional objects no one of which could be uniquely specified by alternative conditions that fail of logical equivalence.

I am unable to construct a plausible argument that the purification suggested by Quine would have such beneficial consequences. At any rate, he was wrong about this and he says so. "As a matter of fact, the worrisome charge that quantified modal logic can tolerate only intensions and not classes or individuals was a mistake to begin with. . . . I have been slow to see it, but the proof is simple."[14] Suppose that the condition 'ψx' uniquely determines the object x. Then, where 'p' is any truth not implied by 'ψx', '$p \cdot \psi x$' also uniquely determines x. But the two conditions 'ψx' and '$p \cdot \psi x$' are contingently and not logically coincident. This argument does not depend upon the extensionality of x, so intensionalizing the values of the variables will not evade it.

Suppose that we go at it the other way around and simply exclude those objects from our domain of discourse which admit of unique specification by conditions which fail of necessary equivalence. "There ceases to be any . . . objections to quantifying into modal position. Thus we can legitimize quantification into modal position by postulating that whenever each of two open sentences uniquely determines one and the same object x, the sentences are equivalent by necessity."[15] We can put this opacity-annihilating postulate thus, where 'Fx' and 'Gx' are arbitrary open sentences and 'Fx and x only' is short for '$(w)(Fw$ if and only if $w = x)$':

(8)   If Fx and x only and Gx and x only, then (necessarily $(w)(Fw$ if and only if Gw)).

But this postulate annihilates modal distinctions along with the referential opacity of necessity. For letting 'p' stand for any true sentence, it can be shown that necessarily p. Let y be any object and let $x = y$. Then

(9)   (p and $x = y$) and x only

and

(10) $x = y$ and x only.

Next, in our postulate take 'Fx' as '$p . x = y$' and 'Gx' as '$x = y$'. It follows from (9) and (10) that

(11)   necessarily $(w)((p$ and $w = y)$ if and only if $w = y)$.

Statement (11) implies '(p and $y = y$) if and only if $y = y$', which implies p. Hence, since what is implied by a necessary truth is a necessary truth, (11) implies that necessarily p. Q.E.D. Modal distinctions collapse.[16]

Here the argument against intensions as values for the variables of quantified modal logic is carried through without consideration of singular terms. But it can be carried through with reference to them as well, according to Quine. The rationale behind the recourse to intensions as values for the variables of quantified modal logic was, in the first place, the consideration that intensions seemed to have the right sort of names for their job. Names for intensions were supposed to satisfy the condition that any two of them naming the same intension would be terms of a necessarily true statement of identity. A modal logic that confines

124

its domain of discourse to intensions would thus be free of referentially opaque contexts.

Intensions, with the obscurity of their identity-conditions, may be, as Quine says, "creatures of darkness." But if the above stated condition on their names is taken as analytic of them, it can be shown that they do not exist at all. The argument is Quine's: "For, where A is any intensional object, say an attribute, and 'p' stands for an arbitrarily true sentence, clearly,

$$(35) \quad A = (\imath x)[p.(x = A)].$$

Yet, if the true statement represented by 'p' is not analytic, then neither is (35), and its sides are no more interchangeable in modal contexts than are 'Evening Star' and 'Morning Star', or '9' and 'the number of the planets'."[17] Objection might arise to this argument on the Russellian grounds that Quine's (35) is not an identity-statement since it contains a definite description. One might maintain that Quine has given an overly liberal interpretation to the condition on designations for intensions. It is not required that *any* designations for the same intension be terms of a necessarily true identity-statement; this is required only of proper names. One might argue even more radically that all of Quine's difficulties in interpreting modal logic, insofar as they turn on the anomalous behavior of singular terms, together with the recourse to intensions, could have been avoided by scrupulous attention to the distinction between proper names and definite descriptions together with the scope distinctions attendant upon the latter. We turn now to consideration of this.

VII

The view was first put forth by A. F. Smullyan.[18] According to Smullyan, sentence (3) is unambiguous—it is analyzed simply as $N(F(y))$, and the identity-premiss (2) has the form $y = (\imath x)$ (φx). But the conclusion (4) is ambiguous, for it can be understood as according the description a primary occurrence, that is, as being of the form

$$(12) \quad [(\imath x) (\varphi x)]\Box\{F(\imath x) (\varphi x)\},$$

or (4) can be understood as according the description a secondary occurrence, that is, as being of the form

(13) $\Box\{[(\imath x)\,(\varphi x)]F(\imath x)\,(\varphi x)\}.$

The distinction is the same as that between an assertion of the form

(14)   The so-and-so satisfies the condition that it is necessary that $F(x)$

and an assertion of the form

(15)   It is necessary that the so-and-so satisfies the condition that $F(x)$.

Here is Smullyan's illustration of the difference:

> I will ask the reader to believe that James is now thinking of the number 3. If, now, someone were to remark 'There is one and only one integer which James is now thinking of and that integer is necessarily odd', then he would be stating a contingent truth. For that there is just one integer James now thinks of, is only an empirical fact. This fact could just as well be expressed in the form [14]. 'The integer, which James is now thinking of, satisfies the condition that it is necessarily odd'. In contrast, the statement, 'It is necessary that James's integer is odd', which is of the form [15], is an impossible statement and not a contingent one. If not necessary then necessarily not necessary: at least, so we assume.[19]

Quine's mistake, according to Smullyan, is to ignore the ambiguity of (4). Quine assumes it to be of the form (13), for he assumes that (4) is false. But understood as exemplifying the form (13), (4) does not follow from the premises. Understood as being of the form (12), (4) does follow by substitutivity; and there is no paradox in this, for thus understood, (4) is true. But is this last contention as clearly true as Smullyan thinks it to be? When the description is eliminated, (12) becomes

(16) $(\exists c)\,(x)\,\{((\varphi x)\equiv(x=c))\&\Box(Fc)\}.$

Smullyan totally bypasses the problem of making sense of such constructions as this. Has Quine not shown that the attempt to bind a variable in a referentially opaque context by a quantifier outside the context produces nonsense? According to Quine, (16) is nonsense, so it cannot represent a possible sense of (4). Thus Smullyan's argument from ambiguity is destroyed. Friends of Smullyan's viewpoint will be quick to answer that Quine's *argument* for the unintelligibility of constructions such as (16) rests on the fallacy of ambiguity exposed by Smullyan. Quine's argument against quantifying into modal contexts assumes the unintelligibility of such constructions as (16), so it begs the question. Smullyan's argument against Quine assumes the intelligibility of these quantifications, but no attempt is made to explain them. Thus Quine and Smullyan can each find the other begging the question at issue. "Notice to begin with," says Quine, "that if we are to bring out Russell's distinction of scopes we must make two contrasting applications of Russell's contextual definition of description. But when the description is in a non-substitutive position, one of the two contrasting applications of the contextual definition is going to require quantifiying into a non-substitutive position. So the appeal to scopes of descriptions does not justify such quantification, it just begs the question."[20] Quine's second reason for rejecting the recourse to the theory of descriptions in defense of modality rests with his theory of the "primacy of predicates." According to Quine, all constant singular terms are eliminable in favor of general terms and bound variables. So if referential opacity is worth worrying about, it must show its symptoms when the constant singular terms are gone. The argument against quantifying into opaque contexts can then still be made. Take the sentence

(17) $(\exists x)$ (necessarily x is odd).

"Let us ban singular terms other than variables. We can still specify things; instead of specifying them by designation we specify them by conditions that uniquely determine them. On this approach we can still challenge the coherence of [17], by asking that such an object x be specified. One answer is that

$$[18] \quad (\exists y)(y \neq x = yy = y+y+y).$$

But that same number x is uniquely determined also by this different condition: there are x planets. Yet [18] entails 'x is odd' and thus evidently sustains 'necessarily x is odd', while 'there are x planets' does not."[21] Statement (18) and 'there are x planets' uniquely specify the same object. Does that object verify (17)? We might answer "yes" if we start from (18) since it entails 'x is odd'. But if we start from 'there are x planets' we will answer "no," since this latter specification does not entail 'x is odd'. Thus we are unable to specify an object which verifies (17). The idea of there being an object which is necessarily odd is incoherent. The only recourse for the modal logician is a doctrine of essentialism according to which (18) is germane to (17), since it specifies its object essentially, while 'there are x planets' specifies that same object accidentally and thus is irrelevant to (17).

Quine's view is that we can make tolerable sense of modal statements, so long as we interpret them relative to particular modes of designating the objects referred to in them. Thus (3) is true of the object 9 relative to its specification by '9', but (4), though it attributes the same property to that object, is false relative to the specification of 9 as 'the number of the planets'. The attempt to attribute necessary properties to objects *an sich* aborts into nonsense. But quantification, ordinarily understood, *abstracts* from the mode in which objects are designated. The statement $(\exists x)F(x)$ is true or false according to whether or not at least one object satisfies the open sentence following the quantifier; but whether or not an object satisfies an open sentence is quite independent of how we refer to it, or even whether we have the means of referring to it at all. Thus there is a fundamental conflict between modality and quantification.

The only (dim) hope for modal logic, Quine thinks, lies in a reversion to "Aristotelian essentialism." He explains, "This means adopting an invidious attitude toward certain ways of uniquely specifying x, for example ['there are x planets'], and favoring other ways, for example [18], as somehow better revealing the 'essence' of the object. Consequences of [18] can, from

128

such a point of view, be looked upon as necessarily true of the object which is 9 (and is the number of the planets), while some consequences of ['there are *x* planets'] are rated still only contingently true of that object."[22] What is required of "Aristotelian essentialism" is that, despite examples like (3) and (4), it provide a sense for the idea of an object, *an sich* and by any name (or none), having some of its properties necessarily and some contingently, regardless of the fact that the former properties follow analytically for that object from certain modes of specifying it just as the latter properties do from other modes of specification. Quantification in modal logic must receive an interpretation that abstracts from the ways in which the values of variables are designated, on pain of not really being quantification at all.[23]

7

Semantics for Modal Logic:
Aristotelian Essentialism

Quine's objections to quantified modal logic come to rest finally on the contention that statements containing bound variables within the scope of a modal operator are unintelligible because of their commitment to what he calls "Aristotelian essentialism." But Quine's criticisms had not been made with reference to a specific class of interpreted formal languages of modality. In this chapter I will first present an account of the semantics of quantified modal logic with the aim of showing how and at what point the involvement with essentialism occurs. I shall then, in the remainder of the chapter, defend quantified modal logic against the charge of unintelligibility. The semantical account of part I follows Saul Kripke's "Semantical Considerations on Modal Logic"[1] and is but a paraphrase and quotation of it.

I

Kripke's paper presents some features of a semantical theory of modal logics, and it is mainly concerned with one aspect of the theory, the introduction of quantifiers.

Four modal systems are considered. Uppercase letters $A, B, C,$ . . . from the upper end of the alphabet represent formulas of the object language and uppercase letters from the lower end of the alphabet $P, Q, R,$ . . . represent atomic formulas. The system M (sometimes called T) has the following axiom schemata and rules:

130

A0.   Truth-functional tautologies

A1. $\Box A \supset A$

A2. $\Box (A \supset B) \supset . \Box A \supset \Box B$

R1. $A, A \supset B \: / \: B$ *modus ponens*

R2. $A \: / \: \Box A$ necessitation (Gödel's rule)

Any modal system which is an extension of M, in the sense that its theorems include all theorems of M, and which is also closed under *modus ponens* and necessitation, is said to be a "normal" system of modal logic.

If we add to M the following axiom scheme, we obtain Lewis' S4:

$$\Box A \supset \Box \: \Box A.$$

We get what is called, following Oskar Becker, the *"Brouwersche"* system if we add the following to M:

$$A \supset \Box \Diamond A.$$

We get Lewis' S5 if we add the following to M:

$$\Diamond A \supset \Box \Diamond A.$$

The displayed axioms are often referred to as the *characteristic* S4, *Brouwersche*, and S5 axioms, respectively. The semantic considerations of Kripke's paper are restricted to normal systems of modal logic, although he has also developed a theory for non-normal systems such as Lewis' S2 and S3.

The first step in the construction of the semantics (model theory) for modal logic requires the introduction of the notion of a (normal) *model structure*. A model structure is an ordered triple $(\mathbf{G}, \mathbf{K}, R)$ where $\mathbf{K}$ is a set, R a reflexive relation defined on $\mathbf{K}$, and $\mathbf{G} \epsilon \mathbf{K}$. Intuitively we think of $\mathbf{K}$ as the set of all possible worlds, $\mathbf{G}$ as the actual world. If $\mathbf{H}_1 \epsilon \mathbf{K}$ and $\mathbf{H}_2 \epsilon \mathbf{K}$, $\mathbf{H}_1 R \mathbf{H}_2$ means that $\mathbf{H}_2$ is "possible relative to" $\mathbf{H}_1$, that is, that every proposition true in $\mathbf{H}_2$ is possible in $\mathbf{H}_1$. Another way of putting it is this: Consider a given possible world $\mathbf{H}_1$ and the totality of propositions which are possible in it. We now consider the set of possible worlds (members of $\mathbf{K}$) which are such that the totality of propositions

131

true in each of them is a compossible subset of those possible in H_1. Each of these latter worlds H' is such that H_1RH', that is, H', is a possible world relative to H_1 or it is *accessible from* H_1.

It is clear, then, why the requirement of *reflexivity* is imposed on R in the definition of a model structure. Whatever is true in H is possible in H, hence H is accessible from itself, HRH. (Sometimes H_1RH_2 is also read "H_2 is an alternative to H_1".) Although reflexivity is the only structural requirement on R in the definition of a normal model structure, we may impose further requirements corresponding to the characteristic axioms of the principal modal system. If R is transitive (as well as reflexive), we call (G, K,R) an S4 model structure; if R is symmetric, (G,K,R) is a *Brouwersche* model structure; and if R is an equivalence relation (reflexive, symmetric, and transitive), we call (G,K,R) an S5 model structure. Without any such restrictions, a model structure is an M-model structure.

We now add the notion of a *model*. Given a model structure (G,K,R), a *model* assigns to each atomic formula (propositional variable) P a truth-value T or F in each world $H \in K$. Formally, a model φ on a model structure (G, K, R) is a binary function $\varphi(P,H)$ where P varies over atomic formulas and H over possible worlds (elements of K), whose range is $\{T,F\}$. In classical propositional logic, φ is what is called an *interpretation*. We now define the assignments of truth-values to nonatomic formulas by recursion. Assume $\varphi(A,H)$ and $\varphi(B,H)$ defined for all $H \in K$. If $\varphi(A,H) = \varphi(B,H) = T$, define $\varphi(A \wedge B,H) = T$; otherwise $\varphi (A \wedge B,H) = F$. $\varphi(\sim A,H) = F$ iff $\varphi(A,H) = T$; otherwise $\varphi(\sim A,H) = T$. And now for the key clause, $\varphi(\Box A,H) = T$ iff $\varphi(A,H') = T$ for every $H' \in K$ such that HRH'; otherwise $\varphi(\Box A,H) = F$. Intuitively A is necessary in H iff A is true in all worlds H' possible relative to H. Kripke has proven the following:

Completeness Theorem

$\vdash A$ in M(S4, S5, the *Brouwersche* system) if and only if $\varphi(A,G) = T$ for every model φ on any M(S4, S5, *Brouwersche*) model structure (G,K,R).

At this stage we have the semantics for (normal) propositional modal logic. We may pause here long enough to illustrate how the

imposition of various structural requirements on the alternative-
ness relation brings out the validity of the characteristic reduc-
tion axioms of the normal systems of modal logic. Consider
transitivity. We want to show that $\Box A \supset \Box \Box A$ is S4 valid, that
is, $\varphi(\Box A \supset \Box \Box A,\mathbf{G}) = \mathbf{T}$ for every model φ on an S4 model
structure $(\mathbf{G},\mathbf{K},\mathit{R})$.

Proof

1. Assume $(A)\varphi(\Box A,\mathbf{G}) = \mathbf{T}$ and $(B)\varphi(\Box \Box A,\mathbf{G}) = \mathbf{F}$ for
   some φ on a model structure.
2. $\varphi(\Box A,\mathbf{H}) = \mathbf{F}$, for some $\mathbf{H}\epsilon\mathbf{K}$, such that $\mathbf{G}\mathit{R}\mathbf{H}$. (B)
3. $\varphi(A,\mathbf{H}') = \mathbf{F}$, for some $\mathbf{H}'\epsilon\mathbf{K}$, such that $\mathbf{H}\mathit{R}\mathbf{H}'$. (2)

Now R is a transitive relation by definition of an S4 model struc-
ture, hence since $\mathbf{G}\mathit{R}\mathbf{H}$ and $\mathbf{H}\mathit{R}\mathbf{H}'$, $\mathbf{G}\mathit{R}\mathbf{H}'$. Hence $\varphi(A,\mathbf{H}') = \mathbf{T}$,
by (A) in contradiction to (3). Hence the assumption (1) is re-
futed and the characteristic S4 axiom is shown to be valid by our
semantics.

We proceed now to the introduction of quantifiers. First we
associate with each $\mathbf{H}\epsilon\mathbf{K}$ a set. Formally, we define a *quantificational model structure* as a model structure $(\mathbf{G},\mathbf{K},\mathit{R})$, together
with a function ψ which assigns to each $\mathbf{H}\epsilon\mathbf{K}$ a set $\psi(\mathbf{H})$ called
the *domain* of $\mathbf{H}$. Intuitively $\psi(\mathbf{H})$ is the set of all things which
exist in $\mathbf{H}$. In general, $\psi(\mathbf{H})$ will not be the same for different
arguments $\mathbf{H}$; intuitively we may expect to see some actually existing individuals absent from other possible worlds and some non-
existing individuals present in them.

We add to our present stock of symbols for propositional
modal logic an infinite list of (individual) variables, the universal
quantifier, and for each non-negative integer n, a list of n-adic
predicate letters P^n, Q^n, . . . (Superscripts may be suppressed
when they may be understood from the context.) Propositional
variables are predicate letters without superscripts, 0-adic. The
notion of a *well-formed formula* is now supposed defined re-
cursively in the usual manner, and we turn to the definition of a
quantificational model on a quantificational model structure.

To define a model (on a model structure) we required a

mapping of ordered pairs of propositional variables and possible worlds into the truth-values, $\{\mathbf{T},\mathbf{F}\}$. Analogously now we suppose that each n-adic predicate letter determines a set of ordered n-tuples which is its *extension* in each possible world. Consider the monadic predicate formula $P(x)$. For each world $\mathbf{H}\epsilon\mathbf{K}$ $P(x)$ is true of some individuals in $\psi(\mathbf{H})$ and false of others; formally $\varphi(P(x),\mathbf{H}) = \mathbf{T}$ relative to certain assignments of elements of $\psi(\mathbf{H})$ to x and relative to other assignments $\varphi(P(x),\mathbf{H}) = \mathbf{F}$. The set of all individuals of which $P(x)$ is true in $\mathbf{H}$ is called its extension in $\mathbf{H}$. But what value should $\varphi(P(x),\mathbf{H})$ have when x is assigned an individual which does not exist in $\mathbf{H}$ but which does exist in some other possible world? Should it have a truth-value at all? Frege and Strawson would not, in this case, assign $P(x)$ a truth-value at all, and Russell, on a natural extension of his views, would assign it the value False.

Kripke chooses not, at this time, to explore these alternatives, but to develop the more classical alternative which excludes truth-value gaps. A statement containing free variables is assumed to have a truth-value at every possible world for every assignment of objects to its free variables, even when these objects do not exist in a world. Formally the position is put as follows: Let $\mathbf{U} = \underset{\mathbf{H}\epsilon\mathbf{K}}{\mathbf{U}}\ \psi(\mathbf{H})$. $\mathbf{U}^n$ is the nth Cartesian product of $\mathbf{U}$ with itself, the set of all n-tuples of elements of $\mathbf{U}$. We define a quantificational *model* on a quantificational model structure $(\mathbf{G},\mathbf{K},\mathbf{R})$ as a binary function $\varphi(P^n,\mathbf{H})$, where the first variable ranges over n-adic predicate letters, for free choice of n, and $\mathbf{H}$ ranges over elements of $\mathbf{K}$. If $n = 0$, that is, for propositional variables, $\varphi(P^n,\mathbf{H}) = \mathbf{T}$ or $\mathbf{F}$; if $n\geq1$, $\varphi(P^n, \mathbf{H})$ is a subset of $\mathbf{U}^n$. We now define a truth-value $\varphi(A,\mathbf{H})$ for every formula A in every $\mathbf{H}\epsilon\mathbf{K}$, with respect to a given assignment of elements of $\mathbf{U}$ to the free variables of A. For $n = 0$, $\varphi(P^n,\mathbf{H}) = \mathbf{T}$ or $\mathbf{F}$. For atomic formulas $P^n(x_1, \ldots, x_n)$, where P^n is an n-adic predicate letter and $n\geq1$, given an assignment of elements $a_1, \ldots, a_n$ of $\mathbf{U}$ to $x_1, \ldots, x_n$, respectively, we define $\varphi(P^n(x_1, \ldots, x_n),\mathbf{H}) = \mathbf{T}$ if the ordered n-tuple $(a_1, \ldots, a_n)\epsilon\varphi(P^n,\mathbf{H})$; otherwise, $\varphi(P^n(x_1, \ldots, x_n),\mathbf{H}) = \mathbf{F}$, with respect to the same assignment.

Given these assignments of truth-values to the atomic formulas, we proceed inductively to assign truth-values for the complex cases of formulas. The steps for the propositional connectives, $\wedge, \sim, \square$, are as given already. Let $A(x, y_1, \ldots, y_n)$ be a formula in which x and the y_i $(1 \leq i \leq n)$ are the only free variables. Assume that a truth-value $(A(x, y_1, \ldots, y_n), \mathbf{H})$ has been defined for each assignment of elements of $\mathbf{U}$ to the free variables of $A(x, y_1, \ldots, y_n)$. We define $\varphi((x)A(x, y_1, \ldots, y_n), \mathbf{H}) = \mathbf{T}$ with respect to an assignment of $b_1, \ldots, b_n$ to $y_1, \ldots, y_n$ (for $b_i(1 \leq i \leq n)$ elements of $\mathbf{U}$), if $\varphi(A(x, y_1, \ldots, y_n), \mathbf{H}) = \mathbf{T}$ for *every* assignment of $a, b_1, \ldots, b_n$ to $x, y_1, \ldots, y_n$, respectively, where $a \epsilon \psi(\mathbf{H})$; otherwise $\varphi((x)A(x, y_1, \ldots, y_n), \mathbf{H}) = \mathbf{F}$ with respect to the given assignment. The restriction $a \epsilon \psi(\mathbf{H})$ requires that we quantify only over objects existing in $\mathbf{H}$.

To see how the semantics works Kripke presents a countermodel for the Barcan formula $(x)\square Ax \supset \square(x)Ax$. We consider a model structure $(\mathbf{G}, \mathbf{K}, \mathbf{R})$, where $\mathbf{K} = \{\mathbf{G}, \mathbf{H}\}$, $\mathbf{G} \neq \mathbf{H}$, and $\mathbf{R} = \mathbf{K}^2$, that is, $\mathbf{R}$ is an equivalence relation so these considerations apply to S5. We extend $(\mathbf{G}, \mathbf{K}, \mathbf{R})$ to a quantificational model structure by defining $\psi(\mathbf{G}) = \{a\}, \psi(\mathbf{H}) = \{a, b\}, a \neq b$. Our countermodel φ is now defined as follows: For a monadic predicate letter P, let $\varphi(P, \mathbf{G}) = \{a\}, \varphi(P, \mathbf{H}) = \{a\}$. Then $\square P(x)$ is true in $\mathbf{G}$ when x is assigned a; and so is $(x)\square P(x)$, since a is the only element of $\psi(\mathbf{G})$. But $(x)P(x)$ is false in $\mathbf{H}$ (since $\varphi(P(x), \mathbf{H}) = \mathbf{F}$, when x is assigned b), hence $\square(x)P(x)$ is false in $\mathbf{G}$. So we have our countermodel for the Barcan formula. Such countermodels can only be removed by imposing the requirement that a model structure satisfy the condition that $\psi(\mathbf{H}') \subseteq \psi(\mathbf{H})$ whenever $\mathbf{H}R\mathbf{H}'$ $(\mathbf{H}, \mathbf{H}' \epsilon \mathbf{K})$. Intuitively the requirement is that as we pass from a possible world to other worlds possible relative to it, no new individual shall come into existence. There are no possible, though nonactual, objects. Kripke also shows that in the present semantics the converse of the Barcan formula is not valid and that the relevant countermodels can only be eliminated by imposing the requirement for each quantificational model structure that $\psi(\mathbf{H}) \subseteq \psi(\mathbf{H}')$ whenever $\mathbf{H}R\mathbf{H}'$. Intuitively this is the requirement that as we pass from a possible world to other worlds possible relative to it, no individual existing in the first world shall pass out of existence. Hence we obtain both the Barcan formula and its converse by requiring that ψ be a constant function which assigns the same domain to all worlds possible relative to a given world.

For any formula A, we define a *closure* of A to be any formula without free variables obtained by prefixing universal quantifiers and necessity signs, in any order, to A. The axioms of the quantificational extension of M are the closures of the following schemata:

(0) Truth-functional tautologies
(1) $\Box A \supset A$
(2) $\Box (A \supset B) . \supset . \Box A \supset \Box B$
(3) $A \supset (x)A$, where x is not free in A
(4) $(x)(A \supset B) . \supset . (x)A \supset (x)B$
(5) $(y)((x)A(x) \supset Ay)$

The sole rule of inference is that of detachment for material implication. Necessitation is a derivable rule.

Quantified extensions of S4, S5, and the *Brouwersche* system are obtained by addition to these schemata of all closures of the appropriate characteristic axiom. All laws of nonmodal quantification theory, modified to admit the empty domain, are theorems in these systems. Kripke has proven semantical completeness theorems for them.

Kripke introduces *existence* as a predicate. Syntactically, existence is a monadic predicate $E(x)$ which can be characterized semantically as satisfying for each model φ on a quantificational model structure, the identity condition $\varphi(E, \mathbf{H}) = \psi(\mathbf{H})$ for every $\mathbf{H} \epsilon \mathbf{K}$. Two axioms are needed regulating existence. He postulates all closures of $(x)A(x) \wedge E(y) . \supset . Ay$ and $(x)E(x)$ as axioms. The statement $\Box(x)E(x)$ is valid, but $(x)\Box E(x)$ is not. Since the converse of the Barcan formula is not valid, this is as it should be.

Identity can be introduced as a binary predicate characterized semantically by defining $x = y$ to be true in a world $\mathbf{H}$ when x and y are assigned the same value, and false otherwise. $\varphi(=, \mathbf{H}) =$

$\{<u,u>:u\epsilon U\}$ for every $H\epsilon K$. If this is done, the predicate of existence is definable, $E(x)$ means $(\exists y)(x=y)$.

II

We now have a precise account of the semantics of a class of formal languages of modality. We can proceed to reexamine Quine's attack on the intelligibility of such languages with this account in mind. We saw in chapter 6 that Quine's attack is double pronged. One prong goes to the irregular behavior of singular terms in modal contexts. We will consider these arguments in this section. The other prong of Quine's attack goes to the intelligibility of statements combining quantifiers and modal operators even after the elimination of all singular terms. These considerations are the subject of section III of this chapter.

Quine's arguments finally come down to the charge that modal logic is committed to essentialism. One symptom of this is found in theorems of modal logic concerning identity and in particular a theorem which actually asserts that all objects have an essential property. The theorem in question is also crucial in the derivation of the modal paradoxes involving singular terms. Quine says, "The system presented in Miss Barcan's pioneer papers on quantified modal logic differed from the system of Carnap and Church in imposing no special limitations on the values of variables. That she was prepared, moreover, to accept essentialist presuppositions seems rather hinted in her theorem

$$(x)(y)\{(x=y) \supset [necessarily(x=y)]\},$$

for this is as if to say that some at least (and in fact at most; cf. 'p . Fx') of the traits that determine an object do so necessarily."[2] The above law has indeed been the focus of much distrust of our subject and I want to examine it in this light.

A necessary statement is, according to our semantics, one which is true in every possible world and a contingent statement is one which is true in some but not all possible worlds. But there seems to be a straightforward argument which shows that all true identity-statements are necessary truths. First, the law of the substitutivity of identity says that if x is identical with y, then if x has any property F, so does y:

$$(1) \quad (x)(y)[(x=y) \supset (Fx \supset Fy)].$$

Every object is necessarily identical with itself:

$$(2) \quad (x)\Box(x=x).$$

A substitution instance of (1) yields

$$(3) \quad (x)(y)[(x=y) \supset \{\Box(x=x) \supset \Box(x=y)\}].$$

From (2) and (3) we derive

$$(4) \quad (x)(y)[(x=y) \supset \Box(x=y)].$$

With (4) it seems that we have derived the paradoxical result that all true identity-statements are necessary truths. But surely there are contingent identity-statements! Let $a=b$ be one of them. From (4) we immediately derive $\Box(a=b)$, so $a=b$ is not after all only contingently true. This is our paradox.

Let us examine the steps by which this paradoxical conclusion was reached. Notice first that (4) does not even appear to say that there are no contingent identity-statements; it does not mention statements at all. What (4) says is that whatever is identical with x is necessarily identical with x. But, of course, only x is identical with x, whatever x may be. Hence (4) amounts to no more than (2), everything is necessarily self-identical, and surely it does not follow from this that there are no contingent identity-statements. How could (4) be understood as ruling out contingent identity-statements? Consider our case of $a=b$. If this is an identity-statement, as we assumed, then 'a' and 'b' must be closed singular terms. And if we are to *derive* $\Box(a=b)$ from $a=b$ in accordance with (4), then $(a=b) \supset \Box(a=b)$ must follow from (4) by instantiation. But $(a=b) \supset \Box(a=b)$ thus follows from (4) only if 'a' and 'b' are terms which do not change their denotations from possible world to possible world, that is, 'a' and 'b' must be terms which denote rigidly. If the singular terms which replace bound variables by instantiation are allowed to be non-rigid, then obviously we could have the situation in which $a=b$

138

is true in the actual world but false in some alternative possible world. Thus our semantics would legitimize the inference of false conclusions from true premisses (granting the truth of (4)).

Hence, what (4) really establishes is that any true statement of the form $a=b$, where 'a' and 'b' are rigid designators, is necessarily true. This is something quite different from the conclusion that every true identity-statement is necessarily true. Consider Frege's example, 'Venus = the morning star'. It is, one might contend, both true and contingent and an identity-statement. After all, in some possible world Venus is not the morning star. Those determined to stand by Russell's theory of descriptions will contend that 'Venus = the morning star' is both true and contingent but not an identity-statement, because it contains a definite description. When this description is eliminated from the statement, we see that it has the logical form of an existentially generalized conjunction, and that the identity-sign stands between bound variables. Hence it does not follow from the truth of 'Venus = the morning star' and (4) alone that □(Venus = the morning star). For Russellians, no statement containing a definite description is an identity-statement, and they will understand the claim that there are no contingent identity-statements as compatible with the claim that statements of the form $(\imath x)(\varphi x)=(\imath x)(\psi x)$ are contingent truths.

We have seen that every true statement of the form $a=b$ is a necessary truth if 'a' and 'b' are rigid designators. Among rigid designators some are definite descriptions, for example, 'the integer between 5 and 7', 'the smallest even prime number'. If we adhere to Russell's theory of descriptions, '2=the smallest even prime number' does not serve as a necessary identity-statement though, of course, it is a necessary truth.

I wrote above that from 'Venus=the morning star' and (4), '□(Venus=the morning star)' does not follow. The principal idea behind Russell's account of definite descriptions is that, in general, statements of the form $\psi(\imath x)(\varphi x)$ cannot be taken to be about $(\imath x)(\varphi x)$, for$(\imath x)(\varphi x)$ is not a proper singular term. Under certain conditions, descriptions behave logically exactly

139

like genuine singular terms. Under these conditions descriptions may freely replace and be replaced by bound variables. In extensional contexts there is only one condition that need be satisfied; it is the condition that the description denote E! $(\imath x)\,(\varphi x)$. So $\psi(\imath x)\,(\varphi x)$ follows from $(x)\psi(x)$, with the added assumption E!$(\imath x)\,(\varphi x)$. Of course, for this inference to be valid when the context is nonextensional, the description must be accorded the broadest possible scope in the conclusion. Let us add the premiss 'E! (the morning star)' to (4). We may then derive

(5)   (Venus=the morning star) $\supset\square$(Venus=the morning star).

This looks wrong because 'Venus=the morning star' is a contingent and not a necessary truth; whether or not it is an identity-statement, in its correct logical form, is from this point of view, a secondary matter. But all difficulties at this point arise from ignoring the scope ambiguities of the consequent of (5). In order for (5) to be correctly derivable from (4) (together, of course, with the propriety premiss 'E!(the morning star)'), 'the morning star' must be accorded the entire consequent of (5) as its scope, that is, the consequent of (5) must have the form

$$[(\imath x)\,(\varphi x)]\square a=(\imath x)\,(\varphi x)),$$

that is, it must have the form

$$(\exists c)[(x)\,(\varphi x\equiv x=c)\,\&\,\square\,(a=c)],$$

so the consequent of (5) does not say that the proposition 'Venus =the morning star' is a necessary truth but only that the object which satisfies the condition *being first among stars appearing in the morning* (namely, Venus) is necessarily itself, namely, Venus. Nobody can object to that.

The point of these last remarks is that (4) does not yield any objectionable results when combined with Russell's theory of descriptions. It does not yield objectionable results, in any case, as far as the issue of contingent identity-statements is concerned. My argument rests upon two considerations: (1) Statements involving descriptions are not identity-statements in Russell's theory. (2) What look to be wrong consequences from (4) to the effect that certain contingent truths involving descriptions are necessary truths are not really consequences at all, but logical illusions due to a failure to consider the scope requirements on descriptions replacing free variables in nonextensional contexts.

So far then, considering only descriptions in Russell's way (as we do throughout this section), we have no reason to object to the thesis that all true identity-statements are necessary truths. Now let us consider identity-statements whose singular terms are not descriptions, and first of all those whose singular terms are proper names.

If we mean what Russell meant by "logically proper name," then the necessity of identity thesis for proper names is obviously correct. The reason is that the meaning of a logically proper name is its denotation, so whenever $a=b$ is true, it means the same thing as $a=a$ and is therefore a necessary truth. Kripke's thesis is much stronger than this, for he holds that true statements of the form $a=b$ are necessary truths when 'a' and 'b' stand for ordinary proper names and this is a thesis about natural languages. Russell would have said that 'Hesperus=Phosphorus' is a contingent truth because he regarded ordinary proper names as disguised descriptions. Kripke rejects this part of Russell's theory, maintaining that ordinary proper names are not disguised descriptions or synonymous with descriptions; they are rigid designators. If ordinary proper names are rigid designators, then every statement of the form $a=b$ is a necessary truth, if true at all, when 'a' and 'b' are replaced by ordinary proper names. Kripke maintains this, so once again our question is 'Are ordinary proper names rigid designators?'

Kripke's lectures contain some arguments to refute the thesis that ordinary proper names are not rigid designators, but it is harder to discover some positive reasons for saying that they are. First, for arguments of the first kind. Consider 'Hesperus= Phosphorus'. This certainly expresses an empirical discovery on my part. I wake up one fine morning and am told that that bright object out in the heavens is Phosphorus. On another occasion, in the evening, someone else points to a heavenly body and tells

141

me that it is Hesperus. Perhaps only years later do I discover that they are one and the same planet. Now the argument goes, this is an empirical discovery hence it cannot be an *a priori* truth that Hesperus=Phosphorus, hence this cannot be a necessary truth either. Hence, since it *is* true, 'Hesperus' and 'Phosphorus' cannot be rigid designators. Kripke maintains that 'Hesperus=Phosphorus' is a necessary truth which I have come to know *a posteriori*. Now, it is not disputable that I can come to know necessary truths empirically. Furthermore, 'Hesperus=Phosphorus' and 'Cicero=Tully' are truths which we could not come to know except *a posteriori*. It is this fact which has led to the nearly universal belief that these sentences do not express necessary truths. But that is really a quite paradoxical conclusion. Is there a possible world in which Cicero (that is, Tully) is *not* Tully? That could only be a world in which Cicero is not Cicero, and that is unintelligible.

Kripke's analysis of this conceptual logjam is that it arises from the identification of the *a priori* and the necessary, the *a posteriori* and the contingent. He argues, as we have seen, that these two distinctions are independent. This leaves us free to recognize 'Hesperus=Phosphorus' and 'Cicero=Tully' as *both* necessary and *a posteriori*. Hence, ordinary proper names are rigid designators.

Where does all of this take us with Quine's paradoxes of modal logic? Those of his arguments turning on singular terms turn out to be scope fallacies since they all involve definite descriptions. They are not illustrative of failure of substitutivity of identity in modal contexts because they involve no identity-premiss. All genuine identity-statements are necessarily true, if true at all.

III

To obtain a countermodel for the Barcan formula, Kripke defined a quantificational model on a quantificational model structure in which the (open) sentence $\Box P(x)$ is true in the actual world **G** when assigned the object *a,* because $P(x)$ is true in both **G** and **H** under this assignment. Intuitively, this is to say that *a* falls under the extension of *P* in **H** and in **G**, that is, in all possible worlds. Thus our intuitive interpretation of Kripke's semantics makes crucial use of the idea of one and the same individual existing in different possible worlds. If quantified modal logic is to be of interest, there must be a distinction between necessary properties, properties that an object has in all possible worlds, and contingent properties which it has in some but not all possible worlds.

How then is an object to be identified across possible worlds? There is a problem here because the properties of objects change from possible world to possible world but not all of them change. An answer to the question 'How are individuals to be identified across possible worlds?' must, it would seem, refer us to those properties which the relevant individuals have in all possible worlds in which they exist, for surely we identify individuals by their properties. But, of course, not all necessary properties, thus defined, can be of use in providing a criterion of crossworld identification. In particular, necessary properties which are common to all or to several individuals will not serve to distinguish one individual from others.

It seems that we have no alternative but to fall back on some variety of essentialism. If an object's essential properties are those which it has in all possible worlds in which it exists, our search for a criterion of transworld identification is a search for some subset of these necessary properties which it and it alone has, its individual essence.

If the individual essence of a thing is some property or set of properties which it and it alone possesses in every possible world in which it exists, there does not seem to be any difficulty about specifying some such properties, for this can be done quite trivially. One such property of the object *a* is being identical with *a*. It has already been observed that not any necessary property of an individual will serve the purpose of transworld identification. We now see that some essential properties are useless for this purpose as well. It would be fatuous to suggest that one can pick out an object across possible worlds by finding the object identical with it in each possible world; our problem is how to do that. Here, I think, we can see that two issues must be clearly separated which have not been in much of the discussion of this topic. When we ask for a criterion of transworld identification, it is sometimes assumed that what is at issue is epistemological. How can we discover the same individual from world to world under the ever-changing disguise of its altering properties? The essentialist answer must be to look for the individual essence, where this is conceived to be some set of qualities which we are required to recognize in order to know who we are looking at beneath the disguise. But now, do we really have to have an answer to this epistemological question at all in order to make sense of possible world semantics for modal logic? I think not. What is certainly required is that we make sense of the idea of one and the same individual in different possible worlds; the idea of crossworld identity. We need not supply an answer to the epistemological question 'How would we identify the same individual in different possible worlds?', but we do need to supply an answer to the metaphysical question 'What does it mean to say that an individual is the same in different possible worlds?'

It is important to distinguish between the epistemological question of identification and the metaphysical question of transworld identity, because the critics of quantified modal logic have cited the difficulty of the epistemological question to the discredit of modal logic. On the other hand, the metaphysical question, which is the only one of the two which needs answering if modal logic is to make sense, is not at all hard to answer. We have in fact already answered it. An object, in one possible world, is identical with an object in any other possible world if and only if the second object has all of the necessary properties of the first, including, of course, the first object's property of being identical with the first object. This is to say that the metaphysical question has a trivial answer, and that the so-called problem of transworld identification poses no threat to the intelligibility of quantified modal logic.

The problem of how an object's essential properties can be made to yield an epistemological criterion for transworld identification is not a problem that we propose to even attempt to solve here; certainly Kripke undertook no such task in his papers on the semantics of quantified modal logic. It is not a logical problem at all but an epistemological one. It cannot reasonably be maintained that in the absence of its solution we lack an intuitive understanding of the semantics of quantified modal logic. If to be committed to the intelligibility of the idea of the transworld identity of objects is to be committed to essentialism, then modal logic, in the style of Kripke, is indeed committed to essentialism. Quine, of course, never posed the problem of essentialism in this way; his main work on the topic antedates the work of Kripke. Nevertheless, the work of Kripke and others on the semantics of quantified modal logic has, in a sense, vindicated Quine's claim that quantified modal logic is committed to essentialism. We cannot understand this work unless we can make sense of essentialism in the form of the idea of one and the same individual in different possible worlds. Quine has seen this. He says, in the course of remarks on a paper by David Kaplan, "In any event Kaplan and I see eye to eye, negatively, on essentialism as applied to particulars. The result is that we can make little sense of the identification of particulars across possible worlds."[3] This, of course, is only one sense of "essentialism" and "commitment." Terence Parsons,[4] following Ruth Marcus,[5] has sought the essentialist commitments of modal logic elsewhere, among its theorems (valid sentences). He distinguishes between grades of essentialist involvement, vicious from benign essentialisms, and he shows that the more vicious the essentialism the less the commitment; but again, he is concerned only with the theorems of modal logic. I have no quarrel with him, for his findings are completely compatible with mine.

We have a sense, then, in which modal logic is committed to essentialism. But I think it is clear that we need not accept Quine's conclusion: "So much the worse for quantified modal logic."[6] Having concluded that quantified modal logic entails essentialism, Quine rejects it, because for him essentialism is a nonsensical metaphysical doctrine. But we must distinguish between the claim that we are unable to state a satisfactory explicit criterion which will effectively resolve questions as to whether or not two individuals in different possible worlds are the same individual, and the claim that we are unable to make sense of such identifications at all. The latter claim is not entailed by the former and it is false. Further, it is not entirely clear what a criterion for identification is supposed to be. Our inability to articulate a clear, explicit, criterion (whatever exactly that is) for the reidentification of individuals through time in the actual world does not entail our inability to make such reidentifications successfully. And it is a plain matter of fact that we do regularly succeed in making them.

Suppose someone tells us, 'I did not miss this morning's lecture, but I might have'. The intelligibility to us of this statement depends upon our ability to make sense of the idea that the subject of the statement is identical with an individual in another possible world, one in which he missed this morning's lecture. Indeed the statements, 'I did not miss this morning's lecture, but I might have', and 'I did not miss this morning's lecture, but there is a possible world in which I did' are full paraphrases of each other. The latter statement explicitly identifies its subject with an individual in another possible world; if this makes no sense to us, neither does the former statement. But the former statement does make sense. Our ordinary daily communication is full of statements about what nearly took place, about what might have been the case, about counterfactual situations, about actual individuals in nonactual situations. It is *prima facie* absurd to suggest that all of this is involved in an unintelligible metaphysics. We have surely seen with our own eyes, for example, a person nearly get hit by a car. How can we deny that we understand the statement, 'He nearly got hit'? To the extent that we understand such assertions we are able to make sense of the idea of identical individuals in different possible worlds, for example, of the idea of another possible world in which this very person *is* hit by that very car. This understanding is all that is required to give intuitive sense to the semantics of quantified modal logic. So much the better for quantified modal logic!

I am claiming that we can and do make sense of the idea of one and the same individual in different possible worlds and

146

that we can and do know how to identify individuals across possible worlds. I am appealing to the fact that we understand, and sometimes know to be true, counterfactual statements such as 'He nearly got hit by that car'. I am convinced however, that some philosophers who have discussed these questions and have found the problem of transworld identification (metaphysical change) an insuperable one for the intelligibility of the semantics of quantified modal logic have worked themselves into their position by themselves asking wrong or confused questions. Kripke observes that philosophers sometimes have spoken about possible worlds as though these were distant countries or other planets, and as though the problem of transworld identification was the problem of locating an individual in a distant place when all we had to go on was something like a police description gathered by the authorities from those who knew him here before he left for those distant parts. If you do think about it this way you will suppose that perhaps he has grown a beard and dresses like a woman, or perhaps has changed his sex—after all he has not gone to Japan but much farther, to another possible world; he might even be an Oscar Mayer wiener there. Then how would you know who he was, even if, in this other possible world, "he" were right in front of your eyes?

I think that these are pseudoproblems and I do not think that we need answers to them in order to understand quantified modal logic. Just try to make sense of these questions in the concrete cases I have been considering. Suppose I repeat to you 'He nearly got hit!' I've already said that I regard it as a purely accidental fact about current English usage that I did not say 'In another possible world, very like the actual world, he was just hit by a car!' Now if you are one of those philosophers who is confused about these matters in the way I have described, you will say something like this: 'How do you know that the person in this other possible world, who, unlike the person in the actual world, was hit by the car, is the same person as the unhit person of the actual world?' But what sense am I now to make of your question? It is exactly as though you had asked me instead 'How do you know that it was *he* who nearly got hit by that car?' But I just told

147

you that I was standing there and saw it happen right in front of my eyes—the swerving car, the screeching brakes, his sudden terror and backward lurch. What do you mean, how do I know it was he who was nearly hit? The only sense I can give to your question is to suppose that you are suggesting that I might have been deceived, that the person who nearly got hit was not he, but someone cleverly disguised to look like him in order to deceive me into making this mistaken claim. But then, of course, this is a problem about identification in this world. Once I have identified the person in this world, I do not have to do it again for some possible world in which he is hit, for I have done that at the same time.

What I am suggesting here is a partial answer to the question, 'How can we identify individuals across possible worlds?' The way I know that this individual is identical with an individual in another possible world, very like this one, is by seeing that he nearly got hit by a car. It does not at all follow from this that every counterfactual speculation is intelligible. I do not think that it makes senses to suppose that he might have been an Oscar Mayer wiener! I think he could not have been an Oscar Mayer wiener; in more philosophical language, a person is "essentially" not a wiener, and if you ask how I know that, I would say that it is a necessary truth that I know *a priori*. Nothing in this world which is a person is a wiener in another possible world. Such claims, of course, commit me to some doctrine of essentialism. I am claiming, for example, that every person is essentially a person, a person in every possible world in which he exists, hence a wiener in no possible world. This does not distress me, for such statements as 'He might have been hit by that car, but he could not have been a wiener', though essentialist, seem to me to be about as certain as anything we can claim to know. I cannot see why anyone should regard them as unintelligible metaphysics. Further, I hold that quantified modal logic is committed to the intelligibility of such statements and hence to the intelligibility of such essentialism. I cannot see why any of this should be a source of embarrassment to the friends of quantified modal logic.

When challenging the legitimacy of quantified modal logic we may be confronted with examples such as 'He nearly was hit by that car!', which is clearly intelligible. When defending the intelligibility of quantified modal logic we may be confronted with examples such as 'Socrates could not have been nonhuman', which seems somehow problematic. There is no doubt that we are committed to the intelligibility of assertions such as this latter one by the possible world semantics for modal logic. There we invoke the idea of the totality of the possible worlds in which an individual exists. This implies some exclusion, those worlds in which that individual could not exist. Does the totality of possible worlds in which a person exists contain worlds in which that person's parents are other than those he has in the actual world? In other words, might a person have had parents other than his actual parents? Again, this desk is made of wood but might it have been made from ice frozen from water taken from the Thames? These examples are Kripke's.[7] He says that this desk could not have been made of ice from the Thames; that no person could have had parents other than his actual parents. I find Kripke's views acceptable intuitively. The idea in the case of the desk is not, of course, that in place of that desk there might not have been a desk which looked exactly like it made of ice, but *that* desk (given that it is made of wood) could not have been made of ice. It could have been painted brown (let us assume that it is painted black), but it could not have been made of ice. I have said that I find these views of Kripke correct in these individual cases, but I do not know how to defend them against someone who finds them wrong or devoid of sense.

It is at this point that the opponents of modal logic can make their strongest case. The issue turns on the intelligibility of such assertions about tables and persons. But how does one argue about what makes sense? Let us look again at the two kinds of examples we have considered. They differ importantly and relevantly for the present issue. With examples such as 'Nixon might have lost the election of 1968' or 'He nearly was hit by that car', we treat possible worlds as alternative futures to the actual course of events as they have occurred up to a given point in time. Our history might have been the same as it actually had been up until 1968, at which point instead of the actual course of events which from that point of reference was the future course of events there ensued another future course of events differing from the actual one, at least in the respect that Nixon lost the 1968 election. From the point of reference of any given moment of time, we may consider any number of futures differing from the actual one. We can defend a claim that such alternative futures exist by citing known laws or just commonly accepted beliefs. Nixon, for example, might have decided to debate Humphrey on national television and that might have hurt his chances, as happened when Nixon debated Kennedy.

The contentions that Nixon might not have had parents other than his actual ones, and that this desk could not have been made of ice, are not subject to this alternative-futures interpretation. We cannot envisage Nixon the same as he was up to a certain point in time, then going into some nonactual future to that moment to pick up another set of parents and similarly for the desk. These examples turn on the origin of the objects themselves. They retain a temporal character, of course. Could these things have had origins different in the relevant respects? Kripke's answer is that they could not. But why not? The inability of the essentialist to provide a principled defense of his position on this question must leave a cloud of suspicion and this is, I think, the strongest argument in the antimodalist's arsenal. This is not the problem of transworld identity but certainly rather like that problem, so that one may suspect that it is the real issue not clearly perceived by those who leveled the charge that quantified modal logic was shipwrecked on the reef of transworld identity.

I am distinguishing two kinds of essentialist claims, or degrees of essentialist involvement, with the two kinds of examples. 'Nixon might not have been elected in 1968' is a contention which can be challenged and defended by appeal to facts in a well-known and established fashion. Such claims are argued and regularly settled by reasonable people. But there are no commonly accepted facts or scientific laws that are even relevant to the issue of whether this desk could have been made of ice or whether a person could have had different parents. (For purposes of clarity, let us mean the ovum and sperm by "parents.") All we seem to have to fall back on in these considerations is an intuition of essence.

There is yet another source of metaphysical involvement in Kripke's semantics which should be considered. In constructing his countermodel for the Barcan formula Kripke defined a model structure in which new individuals "come into existence" as we move from the actual world to alternative possible worlds. To maintain the formula we must disallow such models. The Barcan formula can itself be understood to assert that there are no possible but nonactual individuals. The formula has maintained a central place in the issue over the intelligibility of quantified modal logic because this problem seemed so resistant to solution. At this point the antimodalist offers his diagnosis. The issue is another symptom of the metaphysical morass which engulfs modality. What then is the problem of possibilia? The *locus classicus* for this issue is this passage by Quine. "Take, for instance, the possible fat man in that doorway; and, again, the possible bald man in that doorway. Are they the same possible man, or two possible men? How are we to decide? How many possible men are there in that doorway? Are there more possible thin ones than fat ones? How many of them are alike? Or would their being alike make them one? . . . Or finally is the concept of identity simply inapplicable to unactualized possibles? But what sense can be found in talking of entities which cannot meaningfully be said to be identical with themselves and distinct from one another?"[8]

The issue over possible objects is, apparently, individuation. But the source of Quine's problems here seems to be the same misleading conception as the one which produced the pseudo-problem of transworld identity. To say that there is a possible fat man in that doorway is just to say that in some possible world there is a fat man in that doorway. And to say that there is a possible bald man there is to say that in some possible world there is a bald man there. Now Quine asks, "Are these possible men the same or different?" The picture we get is that some kind of investigation or search procedure is required when we do not even know what we are looking for. But it is not a matter of looking for anything. The counterfactual situation (possible world) which I am contemplating is given as one in which there is a fat man in that doorway, or one in which there is a bald man there as well, or one in which there is just one man, both fat and bald. I decide which is the case, I do not discover this. I can consider any of these situations I choose to consider. I tell you what they are. The question whether the fat man and the bald man are the same or not is just the question, "What counterfactual situation are you considering?" It demands a decision not a demonstration. Quine asks, "Is the concept of identity simply inapplicable to unactualized possibles?" Of course it is applicable. But when I describe a possible world I decide how many possible objects I am considering. There is simply no room for the question how I know how many that is. The problem of the individuation of possibilia is another pseudoproblem of a piece with that of cross-world identity. In Kripke's words, "possible worlds are *stipulated, not discovered.*"[9]

Appendix

Two Concepts of Quantification[1]

I

If I say, 'Blue does not exist', I am thinking just of Blue. . . .
It is as if the blue must have being in the first place, before
we can raise the question of its being (Sein) *or non-being*
(Nichtsein).[2]

According to Meinong, "pure objects" are "beyond being and
nonbeing" (*jenseits von Sein und Nichtsein*). Views in this tradition (for example, Russell, *Principles of Mathematics,* 1903)
distinguish between *being* and *existence* so that some things that
are do not exist. Meinong went further. After distinguishing objects which subsist from those which exist, he allowed that objects
might or might not be in either sense so that "there are objects
of which it is true that there are no such objects."[3]

The treatment of existence in the quantificational logic developed subsequent to these writings of Russell and Meinong
is opposite in tendency. Existence is here expressed by the quantifier which is meant to cover all there is. Quine's view on the topic
is widely shared. According to him, there is, of course, a distinction between, say, animals which exist in space and time
and numbers which do not, but this merely reflects a difference
between animals and numbers and argues no ambiguity in
'exists'.[4] Expressing existence with a quantifier, classical first-
order logic implements Kant's view that 'existence' is not a
predicate. We may, of course, introduce '*E*' as a predicate-con-
stant of existence and assign a proper subset of the domain of
interpretation as its denotation. A reason for not doing that is

153

that, assuming with Quine the univocality of 'exists', we wish to avoid mystifications such as $(\exists x) \sim Ex$, that is, "There exists something such that it does not exist."

Quantification theory differs from grammar about the predicative status of 'exists', but Meinong and the early Russell take grammar as a reliable reflection of the logical status of existence as an attribute. It is still open for someone to maintain that quantification theory is compatible with the doctrine of the varieties of being because of ambiguity in the quantifiers.

Carnap (in conversation) gave this argument for univocality of the quantifiers. The existential quantifier just generalizes disjunction, so if it is ambiguous, disjunction is too. But it is absurd to think that 'v' in '$(2 + 2 = 5)$ v $(2 + 2 \neq 5)$' has a different sense from the one it has in '(Los Angeles is a large city) v $\sim$ (Los Angeles is a large city)'. One could as well argue that '$\sim$' has different senses in these statements. The parallel argument holds for universal quantification, replacing disjunction by conjunction.

Identification of quantification with generalized truth-functions calls for infinite conjunctions and disjunctions in infinite domains. Waiving any difficulties that may lurk in this, a consideration against the identification seems to arise from a result of Tarski[5] and Gödel[6] according to which there exist languages which are simply consistent and ω-inconsistent. In such a language, with the natural numbers as the domain of interpretation, Fx is provable for every substitution of a natural number numeral for 'x' and $(\exists x) \sim Fx$ is provable as well. So each disjunct of the infinite disjunction whose generalization has been proven is refuted. We should not view this as refuting the identification thesis for these cases. Rather what has been shown is that ω-inconsistent languages contain false theorems, in spite of their (simple) consistency.

There is nothing in the interpretation of quantifiers as generalized truth-functions which entails their univocality. What follows is only that if quantifiers are ambiguous, so are the other logical constants. A principal thesis of intuitionist logicians is that these constants do vary in meaning when we pass from statements about finite classes to the infinite domains of mathematics.

That is why, they say, classical laws are no longer valid for mathematical reasoning. Certainly this ambiguity is different from the Meinongian, but there is really nothing in the standard interpretation of quantification which rules out Meinong's doctrine of varieties of being.

Quine has long argued against the ambiguity of quantifiers. Grant that the existential quantifier means simply "there exists." How can it be shown that the sense of 'exists' conveyed by it in $(\exists x)(x$ is a prime number) is the same or different from the sense it conveys in $(\exists x)(x$ is a cow)? How can it be shown that the spatiotemporal connotation of the second statement, which is absent from the first, arises from difference in the meanings of 'cow' and 'prime number' rather than the ambiguity of $(\exists x)$?

It is hard to see what could count as evidence in this dispute, though large-scale considerations of theory might incline us in one or the other direction, as Quine later saw.

> There are philosophers who stoutly maintain that 'true' said of logical or mathematical laws and 'true' said of weather predictions or suspects' confessions are two usages of an ambiguous term 'true'. There are philosophers who stoutly maintain that 'exists' said of numbers, classes, and the like and 'exists' said of material objects are two usages of an ambiguous term 'exists'. What mainly baffles me is the stoutness of their maintenance. What can they possibly count as evidence? . . . Why not view 'true' as unambiguous but very general, and recognize the difference between true logical laws and true confessions as a difference merely between logical laws and confessions? And correspondingly for existence?[7]

II

Ruth Marcus[8] and others (Quine heard the idea in conversation with Lesniewski[9]) advocate an interpretation of quantification which, Marcus claims, deprives it of ontological import. Her idea is that $(\exists x)Fx$ is to be interpreted as saying "Some substitution instance of Fx is true" and correspondingly, $(x)Fx$ is to be read "every substitution instance of Fx is true."[10] Nothing, on this

155

interpretation, restricts substitution classes relevant to quantification to the category of singular terms. No dubious ontological implications lurk in such constructions as $(\exists p)p$, for this interpretation of bound variables does not commit us to taking 'p' as ranging over things in that sentence. As Quine says, "Moreover, substitutional quantification makes good sense, explicable in terms of truth and substitution, no matter what substitution class we take—even that whose sole member is the left-hand parenthesis." He cites Lesniewski for the example.[11] Among other advantages of her view of quantification, Ruth Marcus claims that it provides a way out of the singular existence anomalies associated with the standard interpretation. We may wish to claim the truth of

> (1)   Pegasus is a winged horse,

and therefore of

> (2) $(\exists x)(x$ is a winged horse$)$.

Objectual interpretation of the quantifier renders (2) false, so on that interpretation we must renounce (1). But on the substitutional interpretation (2) is true, for the requisite substitution is provided by (1) itself.

The substitutional interpretation obviates controversy over (1) by rendering (2) acceptable. By parity of reasoning it obviates objection to the inference from

> (3)   Pegasus does not exist,

to

> (4) $(\exists x)(x$ does not exist$)$.

So a bonus advantage of the substitutional interpretation, not claimed by Ruth Marcus, is that it affords a clear interpretation of Meinong's doctrine that some objects do not exist.

Substitutional quantification in the substitution class of singular terms is what comes nearest to objectual quantification, but the two are not equivalent. Divergence arises over domains of objects not all of which have names. Then $(\exists x)\ Fx$ may be true objectually, if there is an object in the domain which satisfies Fx, but false substitutionally because no expression of the appropriate substitution class turns Fx true when substituted for 'x'. If every object has a name and every name denotes an object, the divergence disappears, but we are left without a rendering of the concept of existence expressed by the objectual quantifier. According to the objectual view, our discourse is about those objects which fall within the range of values of our bound variables. But substitutional quantifiers do not have ranges or values at all. What Marcus calls "values" of a "variable" are simply members of the appropriate substitution class,[12] and those objects themselves, not their names, are what supplant and are supplanted by substitutional "variables." The substitutional interpretation is blind to the distinction between values and substituends of a variable, a distinction central to the objectual view. The only objects for the substitutionalist are bits of language.

The semantics of classical predicate logic forges an intimate link between reference and quantification. Fa is true if and only if 'a' denotes an object which satisfies the open sentence Fx. $(\exists x)Fx$ is true if and only if *something* satisfies Fx. Thus our semantics validates existential generalization. $(x)Fx$ is true if and only if everything satisfies Fx, so if $(x)Fx$ is true, Fa is too. Thus our semantics validates universal instantiation. The argument for validity of these principles establishes a criterion for singular reference. An expression in a statement is a singular term if and only if it can be *quantified into* its position by universal instantiation and *quantified out* of its position by existential generalization. Failure to preserve truth in the inference from Fa to $(\exists x)Fx$ or in the inference from $(x)Fx$ to Fa has only one explanation: 'a' lacks reference in Fa. To be a singular term is simply and solely to be a substituend for a bound variable.

Substitutional quantification severs this bond between reference and quantification. It is blind to the distinction between referential position and others, for it makes good sense—the same sense—no matter what substitution class we take, even (to repeat Lesniewski's example) the class whose sole member is the left parenthesis. It leaves no way of distinguishing referring expressions from others. If we wish to represent the logic of reference, substitutional quantification is not for us.

III

We have seen in chapter 6 that the price of quantified modal logic is Aristotelian essentialism. But there is a way of evading this cost, for the case there presented was predicated on the objectual interpretation of quantification. Ruth Marcus has urged the substitutional interpretation as providing a clear interpretation of hitherto problematic constructions such as $(\exists x)\Box(x>7)$. And there is certainly nothing obscure about this on the substitution view; it merely says that some substitution for 'x' in $\Box(x>7)$ renders it true and '9' provides the required instance. It has often been suggested that the way to do quantified modal logic is to restrict substitutivity either by placing restrictions on singular terms or by requiring substitution to be supported by a stronger relation than mere contingent identity. Hintikka, for example, proposes a restricted principle of substitutivity according to which terms of a true identity are intersubstitutive only in atomic formulas and identities.[13]

But does any restriction of the application of the principle of substitutivity not make nonsense of quantification? No, for as Dagfinn Føllesdal has pointed out, Hintikka's semantics of quantification is best interpreted as substitutional.[14] This is somewhat obscured by Hintikka's technique of model sets. A model set μ of formulas may be thought of as a partial description of a possible world. A set of (quantificational) formulas is satisfiable if and only if it is embeddable in a model set.[15] Complete sets of conditions which model sets must satisfy are designed to assure this. They can be found in various places, (for example, "Modes of Modality"). Here we are concerned only with the conditions for identity, quantification, and modality. For identity:

(C. self =) μ does not contain any formula of the form
$\sim(a = a)$

(C. =)   If **F** $\epsilon\mu, (a = b)\epsilon\mu$ and **G** is like **F** except for the interchange of a and b at some (or all) of their occurrences, then **G**$\epsilon\mu$ provided that **F** and **G** are atomic or identities.[16]

In order to interpret modal operators Hintikka uses model systems. A model system is a set Ω of model sets ordered by a dyadic relation R and satisfying

(C.N)   If $\Box$**F**$\epsilon\mu\epsilon\Omega$, then **F**$\epsilon\mu$.

(C.M.)   If $\Diamond$**F**$\epsilon\mu\epsilon\Omega$, then there is in Ω at least one μ^* such that $\mu R\mu^*$ and **F**$\epsilon\mu^*$.

(C.N+)   If $\Box$**F**$\epsilon\mu\epsilon\Omega$, then for every $\mu^*\epsilon\Omega$ such that $\mu R\mu^*$, **F**$\epsilon\mu^*$.

The conditions for quantifiers are

(C.E.)   If $(\exists x)$**F**$\epsilon\mu$, then **F**(a/x) and $(\exists x)\Box(a = x)\epsilon\mu$ for some free individual symbol a.

(C.U.)   If (x)**F**$\epsilon\mu$ and $(\exists y)\Box(b = y)\epsilon\mu$, then **F**$(b/x)\epsilon\mu$.

A set of formulas is satisfiable if and only if it is embeddable in a member of a model system.

The condition (C.=) does not guarantee universal substitutivity. Føllesdal has shown that the following denial of substitutivity is satisfiable in Hintikka's semantics[17]:

$$(5) \quad (\exists x)(\exists y)(x = y . Fx . {\sim} Fy).$$

How does Hintikka interpret quantifiers in order to make (5) satisfiable? Føllesdal takes the following,

$$(6) \quad (\exists x)(\exists y)(x = y . \Box Gx . {\sim} \Box Gy),$$

and exhibits a model set containing it:

$$\mu: \ (\exists x)(\exists y)(x = y . \Box Gx . {\sim} \Box Gy)$$
$$(\exists y)(a = y . \Box Ga . {\sim} \Box Gy)$$
$$a = b . \Box Ga . {\sim} \Box Gb$$
$$Ga$$
$$Gb$$

159

$$(\exists x)\Box(a = x)$$
$$(\exists x)\Box(b = x)$$
$$\Box(a = c)$$
$$\Box(b = d)$$
$$a = c$$
$$b = d$$
$$Gc \qquad Gd$$

μ^* (where $\mu R\mu^*$):
$$\sim Gb$$
$$Ga$$
$$a = c$$
$$b = d$$
$$\sim Gd$$
$$Gc$$

Føllesdal's observation on this is that, "The situation is clear as long as we consider only the terms. However, ordinarily a quantifier is interpreted as saying something not about terms but about objects referred to by terms, and one might wonder what happens to the object which in our actual world is the common reference of 'a' and 'b' when we pass into the possible world μ^*. Is this object G or is it non-G in μ^*?"[18]

"The situation," says Føllesdal, "is clear as long as we consider only the terms." Hintikka has long argued that referential opacity is really a matter of referential multiplicity.[19] The reason that '9' and 'the number of planets' are not intersubstitutive in modal contexts, in spite of the fact that they are coreferential in the actual world, is that there are possible worlds in which they are not coreferential. 'The number of planets' suffers from *referential multiplicity*. Thus the explanation of the situation represented by the model sets above is that the terms 'a' and 'b' which refer to the same object in μ refer to different objects in μ^*. Føllesdal's conclusion is that Hintikka's semantic conditions "are conditions on expressions, not on objects referred to by these expressions. And, as we have just observed, it is hard to see how Hintikka's 'substitutional' conditions for the quantifiers can be regarded as conditions on the objects referred to."[20]

So far there is nothing objectionable in Føllesdal's analysis. What is puzzling is his insistence that there is no way of both restricting substitutivity and making sense of quantification, for the arguments against this possibility are all predicated on the objectual interpretation of quantifiers. Føllesdal says, "This [Hintikka's] semantics is incompatible with Quine's thesis. And since the fate of the object referred to by '*a*' and '*b*' in μ remains in the dark, the same difficulties as before arise in connection with the interpretation of the quantifiers."[21] But this cannot be a criticism of the substitutional interpretation. That interpretation is not concerned with the object $a(=b)$ at all, so it cannot be taken as a defect of this view that it fails to account for the fate of that object in the passage from μ to μ^*. One reason that Marcus proposes her interpretation is precisely because that passage is so mysterious.

There is an important difference, relevant to the present discussion, between Hintikka's original set of conditions for model sets in *Knowledge and Belief* and later versions of these conditions. In *Models for Modalities*[22] he abandons the condition

(C.EK $=$)   If '$(\exists x)K_a(x = b)$' is in μ, then '$(\exists x)(x = b)$' is in μ.

This is just to deny that $(\exists x)K_a(x = b)$ (a knows who b is) entails $(\exists x)(x = b)$ (b exists). In justification of this, Hintikka says that this condition fails "in cases where a knows who (or what) someone (or something) is, 'should he (or it) exist', although it so happens that he (it) does not."[23] Now, on the substitutional interpretation, (C.EK $=$) does hold. Assume $(\exists x)K_a$ $(x = b)$. On the substitutional interpretation, it follows that $K_a(c = b)$ is true for some name '*c*'. Hence $c = b$ is true for the same name '*c*'. On the present interpretation $(\exists x)(x = b)$ follows. Q.E.D. Thus the later version of Hintikka's conditions is incompatible with the substitutional interpretation suggested by Føllesdal.[24]

We need not choose between the two concepts of quantification but may use either one or the other as we find convenient. Each existential quantifier corresponds to a different use of 'there is' in ordinary language. The situation calls for Carnap's principle of tolerance, "*In logic, there are no morals.* Everyone is at liberty to build up his own logic, i.e., his own form of language, as he

161

wishes. All that is required of him is that, if he wishes to discuss it, he must state his methods clearly."[25]

IV

The severance of quantifiers from reference attendant upon the substitutional interpretation gives them a freedom of movement they lack in their objectual version. In their paper on the substitutional interpretation, Belnap and Dunn claim as a special advantage of the substitutional view that it legitimizes quantification into quotation.[26] This freedom of quantification into quotation makes possible a truth definition which is a simple generalization of Tarski's paradigm, " 'Snow is white' is true, if and only if, snow is white."

$$(p) (\text{'}p\text{' is true} \equiv p)$$

This is objectionable as a general definition of 'x is a true sentence' because the substituends for 'x' are restricted to quotation names.[27] The definition eliminates the term 'true' from contexts such as ' 'snow is white' is true', but not from contexts such as 'Tarski's paradigm sentence is true'. This restriction is avoided if, exploiting the fact that every (true) sentence has a quotation name, we define truth thus:

(7) $(x)[(x \text{ is a true sentence}) \equiv ((\exists p)x = \text{'}p\text{' } \& p)].$

Quotation is sometimes explained according to the orthographic accident interpretation. On this view, quotation names totally lack logical articulation so that there is no more systematic relationship between ' 'rat' ' and ' 'rational' ' in virtue of the fact that both contain a single pair of quotes than there is between 'rat' and 'rational' in virtue of the fact that both contain the letter 't'. On their objectual interpretation, quantifiers outside of quotations are irrelevant to any variable inside; such a "variable" is simply deprived of its normal role as a singular term. But there is good reason for rejecting the orthographic accident account anyway, because the absence of systematic relationship between quotation names entails that languages with the quotation device have an infinite number of semantically primitive terms. Given some obvious assumptions about the learning capacity of human beings, it follows that such languages are unlearnable.

Tarski discusses another interpretation of quotation which avoids this objection and at the same time legitimizes objectual quantification into quotation.[28] This is the functional interpretation according to which quotation marks are singulary name-forming functors which applied to expressions produce their quotation names. Semantically, these quotation functors denote functions from objects to their quotation names. According to this view, quotation names are logically articulated. "Los Angeles" contains a name, 'Los Angeles', which names an object which, as argument to the quotation function, yields ' 'Los Angeles' ' as value. On the functional view, quotation is a construction so that languages containing an infinite number of quotation names may still contain only a finite number of semantical primitives. The functional view legitimizes quantification into quotation where quantification is understood either according to the objectual or the substitutional interpretation. To see the former, simply consider that on the functional view, the expression inside the quotation marks is a name.

The main difficulty with this view has to do with extensionality.[29] Positions within quotation marks are referential, so names in these positions should be replaceable, *salva veritate,* by co-referential terms, but this is notoriously not the case.

A third view of quotation avoids the objections to these two. According to this view, quotation names are syntactical constructions generated according to the following rule. The result of placing quotation marks around any expression is a (singular) term. So, as against the orthographic accident view, quotation names have a generative history. (Note that the rule allows for nested occurrences of quotation to any depth.) The semantics of quotation is given by the following simple rule. *The denotation of a quotation is the expression resulting from the removal of its outermost pair of quotation marks.* Therefore the quoted expression has no semantically relevant role to play inside the quotation; its reference (if any) is independent of the reference of the quotation name. This makes objectual quantification into quotation senseless. Substitutional quantification into quotation, however, has a clear meaning on this account of quotation. But unless restrictions are imposed, quantification into quotation generates paradox.[30]

Let 'c' be an abbreviation for 'the sentence printed on this page, line 6 from the top'. Let 'S' be an abbreviation of the sentence

$$(p)((c = `p`) \supset \sim p).$$

The quantifier in this sentence is to be read substitutionally, so the sentence has a clear meaning. If we take (7) as a definition of truth, 'S' says that c is not a true sentence, that is, 'S' says that it itself is not true. We use the further evident assumption

(β) $(p)(q)[(`p` = `q`) \supset (p \equiv q)].$

(Again, the sense which the substitutional interpretation accords to (β) renders it true.) We assume, as evident, an empirical premiss

(γ) $c = `S`.$

The antinomy of the liar follows.

(1)	$(p)[(c = `p`) \supset \sim p]$	assumption
(2)	$(c = `S`) \supset \sim S$	1, U.I.
(3)	$c = `S`$	γ
(4)	$\sim S$	2,3,M.P.
(5)	$S \supset \sim S$	1, Con.

We now prove the converse of (5).

(1)	$\sim [(p)((c = `p`) \supset \sim p)]$	assumption
(2)	$(\exists p)((c = `p`) \& p)$	1
(3)	$c = `p` \& p$	2, E.I.
(4)	$c = `p`$	3, simp.
(5)	$c = `S`$	γ
(6)	$`S` = `p`$	4,5, Id.
(7)	$S \equiv p$	β, 6
(8)	p	3, simp.
(9)	S	7,8, M.P.
(10)	$\sim S \supset S$	1, Con.

Two Concepts of Quantification

V

In order to fix our considerations of the subject, a precise formulation of a semantics of substitutional quantification is here appended. Belnap and Dunn's, "The Substitution Interpretation of Quantifiers" is followed throughout.

We are concerned with *standard* or *first-order languages* as usually understood; there is a denumerable infinity of individual variables, predicate letters, perhaps function signs, perhaps individual constants, there are sentential connectives and quantifiers. There are the usual well-formed formulas and terms. Closed terms are *names* and well-formed formulas without free variables are *sentences*.

A *substitution interpretation I* is a mapping of atomic sentences into $\{\mathbf{T}, \mathbf{F}\}$. The *valuation* (with respect to I) v_I is a mapping of the sentences into $\{\mathbf{T}, \mathbf{F}\}$ which satisfies the following conditions:

1. If A is an atomic sentence, $v_I(A) = I(A)$;
2. If $A = \sim B$, $v_I(A) = \mathbf{T}$ iff $v_I(B) = \mathbf{F}$;
3. If $A = B \& C$, $v_I(A) = \mathbf{T}$ iff $v_I(B) = \mathbf{T}$ and $v_I(C) = \mathbf{T}$;
4. If $A = (x)B(x)$, $v_I(A) = \mathbf{T}$ iff $v_I(B(t)) = \mathbf{T}$, for all names t.

Definitions of *valid sentence* and *logical consequence* (for sentences) are as usual.

This is only one of several possible alternative formulations. On another version, for example, atomic sentences (clause 1) can be interpreted in accordance with the classical domain-and-values interpretation without alteration of the other clauses. This is the kind of interpretation Ruth Marcus seems to have in mind in "Modalities and Intensional Languages."[31] In the formulation above, individual constants are not assigned denotations; there is no domain of values. This accords with Marcus' first formulation.[32] Again, clause 4 concerns the substitution class of closed terms (names) exclusively, but it can be adjusted for any substitution class of expressions by fixing the value of 'C' in the following schema:

$v_I((x)A) = \mathbf{T}$ iff $v_I((y/x)A) = \mathbf{T}$ for each member y of substitution class $\mathbf{C}$.

If the substitution class $\mathbf{C}$ is to be that of sentences, then this schema is correct only under the further requirement that the members of $\mathbf{C}$ be of lesser complexity than $(x)A$ itself, and that, in particular, no sentence containing this very quantifier shall belong to $\mathbf{C}$. If the requirement is not imposed our schema fails, through circularity, to provide the truth-condition for $(x)A$, when the quantifier is sentential. Failure to meet this requirement is clearly the source of the paradox derived at the end of the last section. The step from (1) to (2) in the first limb of the argument involves instantiating the quantifier with the very sentence containing it, and is therefore illegitimate according to our requirement.

My aim has not been to demonstrate that there is something incoherent, unintelligible, or otherwise "wrong" with substitutional quantification. What I have wanted to do is only to distinguish it from objectual quantification with which the problems of this book, especially in its second part, are concerned.

Notes

Chapter 1

1. Bertrand Russell, "The Philosophy of Logical Atomism." Reprinted in *Logic and Knowledge,* ed. R. C. Marsh (London: George Allen and Unwin, 1956), p. 243.

2. Russell does not explicitly state this "plausible assumption," but it must be invoked to make his explicit argument valid. Compare, for example, *Principia Mathematica,* vol. 1. 2d ed. (Cambridge: Cambridge University Press, 1925), p. 66. "Whenever the grammatical subject of a proposition can be supposed not to exist without rendering the proposition meaningless, it is plain that the grammatical subject is not a proper name, i.e,. not a name representing some object."

3. Gottlob Frege, "On Sense and Reference," in *Translations from the Philosophical Writings of Gottlob Frege,* ed. P. Geach and M. Black (Oxford: Basil Blackwell, 1952), p. 62.

4. Ibid., p. 58, n.

5. John Stuart Mill, *A System of Logic,* in *John Stuart Mill's Philosophy of Scientific Method,* ed. E. Nagel (New York: Hafner Publishing Co., 1950), p. 26.

6. Saul Kripke, "Naming and Necessity," in *Semantics of Natural Language,* ed. D. Davidson and G. Harman (Dordrecht, Holland: D. Reidel Publishing Co., 1972), p. 277.

7. Frege, "On Sense and Reference," p. 56.

8. Ibid., pp. 56–57.

9. Ibid, p. 57.

10. Bertrand Russell, *The Principles of Mathematics.* 2d ed. (New York: Norton and Co., 1937), p. 449.

Chapter 2

1. Bertrand Russell and A. N. Whitehead, *Principia Mathematica,* vol. 1. 2d ed. (Cambridge, Cambridge University Press, 1925), p. 66.

167

Notes

2. Ibid.

3. Ibid.

4. Ibid., p. 67.

5. Ibid.

6. *Translations from the Philosophical Writings of Gottlob Frege,* ed. P. Geach and M. Black (Oxford: Basil Blackwell, 1952), p. 56.

7. Bertrand Russell, "Descriptions." Reprinted in *Semantics and the Philosophy of Language,* ed. L. Linsky (Urbana: University of Illinois Press, 1952), p. 102.

8. Bertrand Russell, "The Philosophy of Logical Atomism." Reprinted in *Logic and Knowledge,* ed. R. C. Marsh (London: George Allen and Unwin, 1956), p. 243.

9. Jaakko Hintikka, *Models for Modalities* (Dordrecht, Holland: D. Reidel Publishing Co., 1969), p. 27.

10. For this interpretation of Quine's dictum, see Hintikka, *Models for Modalities,* pp. 40–42.

11. Compare Willard Van Orman Quine, *Ontological Relativity* (New York: Columbia University Press, 1969), p. 94.

12. Compare Hintikka, *Models for Modalities,* pp. 30–31.

13. *Translations from the Philosophical Writings of Gottlob Frege,* p. 70.

14. There is a further disadvantage in Frege's method using a^* pointed out by Kalish and Montague. Any language to which it is applied requires the presence of at least one name that is not a description. Hence Quine's program for the elimination of *all* singular terms will be frustrated on this treatment of descriptions. Compare Donald Kalish and Richard Montague, *Logic: Techniques of Formal Reasoning* (New York: Harcourt Brace and World, 1964), p. 264.

15. *Translations from the Philosophical Writings of Gottlob Frege,* p. 69.

16. Alexius Meinong, "The Theory of Objects," in *Realism and the Background of Phenomenology,* ed. R. Chisholm (Glencoe, Ill.: Free Press, 1960), p. 78.

17. Ibid., p. 83.

18. Ibid., p. 82.

19. Ibid.

20. Bertrand Russell, "On Denoting." Reprinted in *Logic and Knowledge,* p. 45.

21. Here I am drawing on unpublished work of Terence Parsons, which he has kindly allowed me to study.

22. Compare Chisholm, *Realism and the Background of Phenomenology,* pp. 10–11.

23. Bertrand Russell, "The Philosophy of Logical Atomism." Reprinted in *Logic and Knowledge,* p. 232.

Notes

24. The theory is presented in the opening passages of "On Denoting" and in *Introduction to Mathematical Philosophy* (London: George Allen and Unwin, 1919), chap. 16.

25. I was stimulated to raise this question by David Kaplan's article, "What is Russell's Theory of Descriptions?", in *Bertrand Russell*, ed. D. F. Pears (New York: Anchor Books, 1972), pp. 227–44. My views about this topic have been greatly influenced by Kaplan's paper.

Chapter 3

1. Saul Kripke, "Naming and Necessity," in *Semantics of Natural Language,* ed. D. Davidson and G. Harman (Dordrecht, Holland: D. Reidel Publishing Co., 1972), pp. 253–355.

2. Ibid., p. 327.

3. Ibid., p. 243.

4. Bertrand Russell, "On Denoting." Reprinted in *Logic and Knowledge,* ed. R. C. Marsh (London: George Allen and Unwin, 1956), pp. 48–51.

5. Kripke, "Naming and Necessity," p. 343, n. 4.

6. Ibid.

7. Ibid., p. 276.

8. Michael Dummett, *Frege: Philosophy of Language* (London: Duckworth, 1973), pp. 112 ff.

9. Kripke, "Naming and Necessity," p. 346.

10. Ludwig Wittgenstein, *Philosophical Investigations* (Oxford: Basil Blackwell, 1953), p. 25.

11. Kripke, "Naming and Necessity," p. 274.

12. Jaakko Hintikka, "Semantics for Propositional Attitudes." Reprinted in *Reference and Modality,* ed. L. Linsky (Oxford: Oxford University Press, 1971), p. 150.

13. Ibid., pp. 150–51.

Chapter 4

1. Michael Dummett, *Frege: Philosophy of Language* (London: Duckworth, 1973), pp. 112–13.

2. Saul Kripke, "Naming and Necessity," in *Semantics of Natural Language,* ed. D. Davidson and G. Harman (Dordrecht, Holland: D. Reidel Publishing Co., 1972), p. 327.

3. Dummett, *Frege: Philosophy of Language,* p. 97. The correspondence to which Dummett refers has not, at the present date, been published.

4. Ibid.

5. Paul Ziff, *Semantic Analysis* (Ithaca: Cornell University Press, 1960), pp. 184–85. Cited by Kripke, "Naming and Necessity," pp. 316–17.

6. Kripke, "Naming and Necessity," p. 317.

7. Ibid.

8. Ibid.

9. Ibid., p. 322.

10. Ibid.

11. Ibid., p. 327.

12. Ibid., p. 316.

13. Ibid.

14. Gottlob Frege, *The Basic Laws of Arithmetic*, trans. and ed. M. Furth (Berkeley and Los Angeles: University of California Press, 1964), p. 90.

15. Hilary Putnam, "Meaning and Reference." *Journal of Philosophy* 70(1973):609–711.

16. My assumption is that we know now that if living beings exist on Mars, they do not share a common biological origin with any living beings on earth.

17. Willard Van Orman Quine, review of *Identity and Individualism,* ed. M. K. Munitz (New York: New York University Press, 1971), in *Journal of Philosophy* 69(1972):492–93.

18. Ludwig Wittgenstein, *Philosophical Investigations* (Oxford: Basil Blackwell, 1953), pp. 36–37.

19. Ibid., p. 37.

20. Kripke, "Naming and Necessity," p. 346, n. 22.

21. Rudolf Carnap, *Meaning and Necessity* (Chicago: University of Chicago Press, 1947), pp. 181–82.

22. The specific citations of Dummett's *Frege* in this chapter do not measure the extent to which its ideas derive from him. Dummett's influence has been pervasive.

Chapter 5

1. Gottlob Frege, "On Sense and Reference," in *Translations from the Philosophical Writings of Gottlob Frege,* ed. P. Geach and M. Black (Oxford: Basil Blackwell, 1952), p. 58, n.

2. John Searle, "Proper Names," *Mind,* n.s., 67(1958):171.

3. Ludwig Wittgenstein, *Philosophical Investigations* (Oxford: Basil Blackwell, 1953), pp. 36–37.

4. Saul Kripke, "Naming and Necessity," in *Semantics of Natural Language,* ed. D. Davidson and G. Harman (Dordrecht, Holland: D. Reidel Publishing Co., 1972), p. 278.

5. Searle, "Proper Names," p. 172.

6. Kripke, "Naming and Necessity," p. 282.

7. Ibid., my emphasis.

8. Keith Donnellan, "Proper Names and Identifying Descriptions," in *Semantics of Natural Language,* pp. 356–79, 373.

9. Kripke, "Naming and Necessity," p. 300.

10. Ibid.

11. Ibid., p. 302.

12. Ibid.

13. Ibid., p. 301.

14. These last remarks are suggested by Michael Dummett, *Frege: Philosophy of Language* (London: Duckworth, 1973), pp. 146–47.

Chapter 6

1. Willard Van Orman Quine, "Reference and Modality," in *From a Logical Point of View*. 2d ed. (Cambridge: Harvard University Press, 1961), p. 139.

2. Bertrand Russell and A. N. Whitehead, *Principia Mathematica*, vol. 1. 2d ed. (Cambridge: Cambridge University Press, 1925), p. 169, *13.01. A complication in the definition deriving from the ramified theory of types is here ignored.

3. Ludwig Wittgenstein, *Tractatus Logico-Philosophicus*, trans. D. F. Pears and B. F. McGuinness (London: Routledge & Kegan Paul, 1961), 5.5302.

4. Quine, "Reference and Modality," p. 140.

5. Ibid., p. 142.

6. Ibid., p. 148. I have adjusted Quine's numbering of sentences to suit the present text.

7. Ibid., p. 156.

8. Gottlob Frege, "On Sense and Reference," in *Translations from the Philosophical Writings of Gottlob Frege,* ed. P. Geach and M. Black (Oxford: Basil Blackwell, 1952), pp. 56–78. Frege never discusses alethic modality in this connection. What is presented here is therefore an application to these cases.

9. Willard Van Orman Quine, "Notes on Existence and Necessity," in *Semantics and the Philosophy of Language,* ed. L. Linsky (Urbana: University of Illinois Press, 1952), pp. 83–84.

10. Quine, "Reference and Modality," p. 140, n.

11. Gottlob Frege, *Foundations of Arithmetic,* trans. J. L. Austin. 2d rev. ed. (Oxford: Basil Blackwell, 1953), p. 73.

12. Cited by Charles Parsons in "Frege's Theory of Number," in *Philosophy in America,* ed. M. Black (Ithaca: Cornell University Press, 1965), p. 182.

13. Rudolf Carnap, *Meaning and Necessity*. 2d ed. (Chicago: University of Chicago Press, 1956), p. 197.

14. Willard Van Orman Quine, *Ways of Paradox* (New York: Random House, 1966), p. 182.

15. Willard Van Orman Quine, *Word and Object* (New York: John Wiley and Sons, 1960), p. 197.

Notes

16. Ibid., p. 198.
17. Quine, "Reference and Modality," pp. 152–53.
18. Arthur F. Smullyan, "Modality and Description," *Journal of Symbolic Logic* 13(1948):31–37.
19. Ibid., p. 31.
20. Quine, "Replies," in *Words and Objections: Essays on the Work of W. V. Quine,* ed. D. Davidson and J. Hintikka (Dordrecht, Holland: D. Reidl Publishing Co., 1969), p. 338.
21. Ibid., p. 339.
22. Quine, "Reference and Modality," p. 155.
23. Much of the present chapter is taken, with permission, from my article "Reference, Essentialism, and Modality," *Journal of Philosophy* 66(1969):687–700.

Chapter 7

1. Saul Kripke, "Semantical Considerations on Modal Logic," *Acta Philosophica Fennica* 16(1963):88–93. Used with the publisher's permission.
2. Willard Van Orman Quine, "Reference and Modality," in *From a Logical Point of View*. 2d ed. (Cambridge: Harvard University Press, 1961), p. 156.
3. Willard Van Orman Quine, "Replies," in *Words and Objections: Essays on the Work of W. V. Quine,* ed. D. Davidson and J. Hintikka (Dordrecht, Holland: D. Reidl Publishing Co., 1969), p. 343.
4. Terence Parsons, "Essentialism and Quantified Modal Logic," *Philosophical Review* 78(1969):35–52.
5. Ruth Barcan Marcus, "Essentialism in Modal Logic," *Nous* 1(1967):91–96.
6. Quine, "Reference and Modality," p. 156.
7. Saul Kripke, "Naming and Necessity," in *Semantics of Natural Language,* ed. D. Davidson and G. Harman (Dordrecht, Holland: D. Reidel Publishing Co., 1972), pp. 313–14.
8. Willard Van Orman Quine, "On What There is," in *From a Logical Point of View*. 2d ed. (Cambridge: Harvard University Press, 1961), p. 4.
9. Kripke, "Naming and Necessity," p. 267.

Appendix

1. Most of this appendix is reprinted, with permission, from *Nous* 6(1972):224–39. © 1972 by Indiana University.
2. Alexius Meinong, "The Theory of Objects," in *Realism and the Background of Phenomenology,* ed. R. Chisholm (Glencoe, Ill.: Free Press, 1960), p. 83.
3. Ibid.
4. Willard Van Orman Quine, "On What There Is," in *From a Logical*

172

Notes

Point of View. 2d ed. (Cambridge: Harvard University Press, 1961), p. 3.

5. Alfred Tarski, "Some Observations on the Concepts of ω-Consistency and ω-Completeness," in *Logic, Semantics, Metamathematics* (Oxford: Oxford University Press, 1956), pp. 279–95.

6. Kurt Gödel, "On Formally Undecidable Propositions of *Principia Mathematica* and Related Systems I," in *From Frege to Gödel*, ed. J. van Heijenoort (Cambridge: Harvard University Press, 1967), pp. 592–616.

7. Willard Van Ormand Quine, *Word and Object* (New York: John Wiley and Sons, 1960), p. 131.

8. Ruth Barcan Marcus, "Interpreting Quantification," *Inquiry* 5(1962): 252–59.

9. Willard Van Orman Quine, *Ontological Relativity and Other Essays* (New York: Columbia University Press, 1969), p. 63.

10. Marcus, "Interpreting Quantification," pp. 252–53.

11. Quine, *Ontological Relativity and Other Essays*, p. 106.

12. Marcus, "Interpreting Quantification," p. 252.

13. Jaakko Hintikka, "Modes of Modality," *Acta Philosophica Fennica* 16(1963):66.

14. Dagfinn Føllesdal, "Interpretation of Quantifiers," in *Logic, Methodology and Philosophy of Science*, ed. B. van Rootselaar and J. Staal (Amsterdam: North Holland Publishing Co., 1968), pp. 271–81.

15. Hintikka, "Modes of Modality," p. 66.

16. Ibid.

17. Føllesdal, "Interpretation of Quantifiers," pp. 277–78.

18. Ibid., p. 278.

19. Jaakko Hintikka, *Knowledge and Belief* (Ithaca: Cornell University Press, 1962), pp. 138–40.

20. Føllesdal, "Interpretation of Quantifiers," p. 278.

21. Ibid., p. 279.

22. Jaakko Hintikka, *Models for Modalities* (Dordrecht, Holland: D. Reidl Publishing Co., 1969).

23. Ibid., p. 134.

24. The argument of this paragraph is due to George Schumm.

25. Rudolf Carnap, *Logical Syntax of Language* (London: Routledge and Kegan Paul, 1937), p. 52.

26. Nuel Belnap and J. Michael Dunn, "The Substitution Interpretation of Quantifiers," *Nous* 2(1968):185.

27. Compare Tarski, *Logic, Semantics, Metamathematics*, p. 159.

28. Ibid., pp. 160–61.

29. Ibid., p. 161.

30. Ibid., p. 162.

31. Ruth Barcan Marcus, "Modalities and Intensional Languages." Reprinted in *Contemporary Readings in Logical Theory*, ed. I. Copi and J. Gould (New York: Macmillan Co., 1967), pp. 278–93.

32. Marcus, "Interpreting Quantification," pp. 252–59.

173

Bibliography

Belnap, Nuel, and Dunn, J. Michael. "The Substitution Interpretation of Quantifiers." *Nous* 2(1968):177–85.

Carnap, Rudolf. *The Logical Syntax of Language.* London: Routledge and Kegan Paul, 1937.

————. *Meaning and Necessity.* 2d ed. Chicago: University of Chicago Press, 1956.

Copi, Irving, and Gould, J., eds. *Contemporary Readings in Logical Theory.* New York: Macmillan Co., 1967.

Davidson, Donald, and Harman, Gilbert, eds. *Semantics of Natural Language.* Dordrecht, Holland: D. Reidel Publishing Co., 1972.

Davidson, Donald, and Hintikka, J., eds. *Words and Objections: Essays on the Work of W. V. Quine.* Dordrecht, Holland: D. Reidel Publishing Co., 1969.

Donnellan, Keith. "Proper Names and Identifying Descriptions." In *Semantics of Natural Language,* edited by Donald Davidson and Gilbert Harman. Dordrecht, Holland: D. Reidel Publishing Co., 1972.

Dummett, Michael. *Frege: Philosophy of Language.* London: Duckworth, 1973.

Føllesdal, Dagfinn. "Interpretation of Quantifiers." In *Logic, Methodology and Philosophy of Science,* edited by B. van Rootselaar and J. Staal. Amsterdam: North Holland Publishing Co., 1968.

Frege, Gottlob. "On Sense and Reference." In *Translations from the Philosophical Writings of Gottlob Frege,* edited by P. Geach and M. Black. Oxford: Basil Blackwell, 1952.

174

————. *The Foundations of Artihmetic.* 2d rev. ed. Translated by J. L. Austin. Oxford: Basil Blackwell, 1953.

————. *The Basic Laws of Arithmetic.* Translated and edited by M. Furth. Berkeley and Los Angeles: University of California Press, 1964.

Gödel, Kurt. "On Formally Undecidable Propositions of *Principia Mathematica* and Related Systems I." In *From Frege to Gödel,* edited by J. van Heijenoort. Cambridge: Harvard University Press, 1967.

Hintikka, Jaakko. *Knowledge and Belief.* Ithaca: Cornell University Press, 1962.

————. "Modes of Modality." *Acta Philosophica Fennica* 16 (1963):65–82. Reprinted in *Models for Modalities.* Dordrecht, Holland: D. Reidel Publishing Co., 1969.

————. "Studies in the Logic of Existence and Necessity: I. Existence." *Monist* 50(1966):57–76. Reprinted in *Models for Modalities.* Dordrecht, Holland: D. Reidel Publishing Co., 1969.

————. *Models for Modalities.* Dordrecht, Holland: D. Reidel Publishing Co., 1969.

————. "Semantics for Propositional Attitudes." In *Philosophical Logic,* edited by J. W. Davis, D. J. Hockney, and K. W. Wilson. Dordrecht, Holland: D. Reidel Publishing Co., 1969. Reprinted in *Reference and Modality,* edited by L. Linsky. Oxford: Oxford University Press, 1971.

Kalish, Donald, and Montague, Richard. *Logic: Techniques of Formal Reasoning.* New York: Harcourt Brace and World, 1964.

Kaplan, David. "Quantifying In." In *Words and Objections,* edited by D. Davidson and J. Hintikka. Dordrecht, Holland: D. Reidel Publishing Co., 1969. Reprinted in *Reference and Modality,* edited by L. Linsky. Oxford: Oxford University Press, 1971.

————. "What is Russell's Theory of Descriptions?" In *Bertrand Russell,* edited by D. F. Pears. New York: Anchor Books, 1972.

Kripke, Saul. "Semantical Considerations on Modal Logic." *Acta Philosophica Fennica* 16(1963):83–94. Reprinted in *Reference and Modality,* edited by L. Linsky. Oxford: Oxford University Press, 1971.

Bibliography

————. "Identity and Necessity." In *Identity and Individuation,* edited by M. K. Munitz. New York: New York University Press, 1971.

————. "Naming and Necessity." In *Semantics of Natural Language,* edited by D. Davidson and G. Harman. Dordrecht, Holland: D. Reidel Publishing Co., 1972.

Linsky, Leonard. *Referring.* London: Routledge and Kegan Paul, 1967.

————. "Reference, Essentialism, and Modality." *Journal of Philosophy* 66(1969):687–700. Reprinted in *Reference and Modality,* edited by L. Linsky. Oxford: Oxford University Press, 1971.

————. "Two Concepts of Quantification." *Nous* 6(1972):224–39.

————, ed. *Semantics and the Philosophy of Language.* Urbana: University of Illinois Press, 1952.

————, ed. *Reference and Modality.* Oxford: Oxford University Press, 1971.

Marcus, Ruth Barcan. "Modalities and Intensional Languages." *Synthese* 13(1961):303–22. Reprinted in *Contemporary Readings in Logical Theory,* edited by I. Copi and J. Gould. New York: Macmillan Co., 1967.

————. "Interpreting Quantification." *Inquiry* 5(1962):252–59.

————. "Essentialism in Modal Logic." *Nous* 1(1967):91–96.

Meinong, Alexius. "The Theory of Objects." In *Realism and the Background of Phenomenology,* edited by R. Chisholm. Glencoe, Ill.: Free Press, 1960.

Mill, John Stuart. *A System of Logic.* In *John Stuart Mill's Philosophy of Scientific Method,* edited by E. Nagel. New York: Hafner Publishing Co., 1950.

Parsons, Charles. "Frege's Theory of Number." In *Philosophy in America,* edited by M. Black. Ithaca: Cornell University Press, 1965.

Parsons, Terence. "Essentialism and Quantified Modal Logic." *Philosophical Review* 78(1969):35–52. Reprinted in *Reference and Modality,* edited by L. Linsky. Oxford: Oxford University Press, 1971.

Putnam, Hilary. "Meaning and Reference." *Journal of Philosophy* 70(1973):609–711.

Quine, Willard Van Orman. "Notes on Existence and Necessity." *Journal of Philosophy* 40(1943):113–27. Reprinted in *Semantics and the Philosophy of Language,* edited by L. Linsky. Urbana: University of Illinois Press, 1952.

————. *Word and Object.* New York: John Wiley and Sons, 1960.

————. *From a Logical Point of View.* 2d ed. Cambridge: Harvard University Press, 1961.

————. "On What There Is." In *From a Logical Point of View.* 2d ed. Cambridge: Harvard University Press, 1961.

————. "Reference and Modality." In *From a Logical Point of View.* 2d ed. Cambridge: Harvard University Press, 1961. Reprinted in *Reference and Modality,* edited by L. Linsky. Oxford: Oxford University Press, 1971.

————. "Quantifiers and Propositional Attitudes." In *Ways of Paradox.* New York: Random House, 1966. Reprinted in *Reference and Modality,* edited by L. Linsky. Oxford: Oxford University Press, 1971.

————. *Ways of Paradox.* New York: Random House, 1966.

————. *Ontological Relativity and Other Essays.* New York: Columbia University Press, 1969.

————. "Replies." In *Words and Objections,* edited by D. Davidson and J. Hintikka. Dordrecht, Holland: D. Reidel Publishing Co., 1969.

————. Review of *Identity and Individuation,* edited by M. K. Munitz. New York: New York University Press, 1971, in *Journal of Philosophy* 69(1972):492–93.

Russell, Bertrand. *The Principles of Mathematics.* 2d ed. New York: Norton and Co., 1937.

————. "On Denoting." *Mind,* n.s., 14(1905):479–93. Reprinted in *Logic and Knowledge,* edited by R. C. Marsh. London: George Allen and Unwin, 1956.

————. "The Philosophy of Logical Atomism." *Monist* 28 (1918):495–527; 29(1919):32–63, 190–222, 345–80. Reprinted in *Logic and Knowledge,* edited by R. C. Marsh. London: George Allen and Unwin, 1956.

————. "Descriptions." In *Introduction to Mathematical Philosophy.* London: George Allen and Unwin, 1919. Reprinted in *Semantics and the Philosophy of Language,* edited by L. Linsky. Urbana: University of Illinois Press, 1952.

Bibliography

Russell, Bertrand, and Whitehead, A. N. *Principia Mathematica,* vol. 1. 2d ed. Cambridge: Cambridge University Press, 1925.

Searle, John R. "Proper Names." *Mind,* n.s., 67(1958):166–73.

Smullyan, Arthur F. "Modality and Description." *Journal of Symbolic Logic* 13(1948):31–37. Reprinted in *Reference and Modality,* edited by L. Linsky. Oxford: Oxford University Press, 1971.

Tarski, Alfred. *Logic, Semantics, Metamathematics.* Oxford: Oxford University Press, 1956.

————. "Some Observations on the Concepts of ω-Consistency and ω-Completeness." In *Logic, Semantics, Metamathematics.* Oxford: Oxford University Press, 1956.

Wittgenstein, Ludwig. *Philosophical Investigations.* Oxford: Basil Blackwell, 1953.

————. *Tractatus Logico-Philosophicus,* translated by D. F. Pears and B. F. McGuinness. London: Routledge and Kegan Paul, 1961.

Ziff, Paul. *Semantic Analysis.* Ithaca: Cornell University Press, 1960.

Index

Index

Conventional kinds, 81
  and phenomenal properties, 81
Counterfactual situations, 53, 74, 146, 152
Criterion of identification, 71, 73, 78–81, 83, 85–87, 90

Daley, Richard J., 91
da Vinci, Leonardo, 55
De dicto/de re, 49–50, 52–55, 58–60, 66, 67, 82
Definite descriptions, xvii, 4, 25–41 passim, 140
  and existence, 3
  and sense, 43, 44
  Frege's theory of, 29–32
  lacking denotation, 46
  logical behavior of, 42–65 passim
  nondenoting, 29
  Russell's theory as regimented model of, 111
  truncated, 23, 45, 47, 50–51, 54
  vacuous, 7, 28
  waste cases of, 27
Definition, 10, 51, 62–63
  contextual, 27, 31, 40, 54, 57, 127
  in use, 19–20
  ostensive, 71, 84–85
Demonstratives, 22
Denotation, xviii, 3–4, 12, 14, 42
  and meaning, 4
Descriptions, indefinite, 39–41
Discourse
  indirect, 8
  serious, 26, 31
Domain, outer, 25
Donnellan, Keith, 105
Dummett, Michael, 54–55, 66–67, 73
Dunn, J. Michael, 162
  on substitutional quantification, 165

Encyclopaedia Britannica, 96

Entity, and identity, 122
Ersatz, for the definite article, 30
Essentialism, xx, 104
  Aristotelian, 120, 128–30, 137, 143, 148, 150, 158
Evaluation procedure, 57–60
  for descriptions, 57–58
  for names, 57–58
Evening Star, 125
Exegesis, 44–45
Existence, 3
  and substitutional quantification, 156
  in modal logic, 136–37
  predicate of, 3, 24, 26, 35, 37–38
  premiss, 26, 46
  property of. *See* Existence, predicate of
Existential generalization, principle of, xix, 4, 24, 26, 31, 119
Extensional contexts, 7, 48

Family resemblances, 75, 76
Fitch, Frederick, 49
Fixing the meaning, 10–11, 51–53, 55, 78, 85
Fixing the reference, 10–11, 51–52, 78, 85
Føllesdal, Dagfinn, 159–60
Form
  and philosophical logic, xxi
  logical, xx
Formal mode of speech, 24, 116
Free variables
  generality interpretation of, 45
  in theorems, 45
Frege, Gottlob, xv–xviii, xxi, 7, 5, 21–41 passim, 42, 51, 68, 70, 74, 87, 93, 95, 120
  on alethic modalities, 171 n 8
  on nondenoting names, 30
  on sense and reference, 21
  on sense of 'Aristotle', 93
Function, partial, 57, 89

Index

Game, 75
General terms, 42, 68
George IV, 63–65
Gödel, Kurt, 154
Gold, 76–77, 79–80
  atomic number of, 79
Goldbach's hypothesis, 91
Grundgesetze der Arithmetik, 30, 32

H_2O, 80
Hesperus, 14, 61, 65, 71–72
Hintikka, Jaakko, 24, 64–65
  on restricted substitutivity, 158, 160–61
Historical theory of names. *See* Causal theory of names
Holy Roman Empire, 9
Homer, 56, 60–61, 63, 66–67, 82–83
  historicity of, 88, 95
Homeric Poems, 96
Humphrey, Hubert, 53, 61

Identity, 116
  across possible worlds, 143–44, 146, 152
    and essentialism, 144–45
    pseudoproblem, 147–49
  conditions, 77
    for sense, 121
  criteria of, xx
    for objects, 35
  in modal logic, 136–37
  necessity of, 138–42
Identity statement, 11–13, 21, 70
  informative, 21–22, 88
Illiad, The 56, 61
Incomplete symbols, 19–23, 37–38
Indefinite descriptions, 39–41
Indiscernibility, principle of, 115
Intensions, 89–90, 123–25
  intensional ontology, 123
Intentionality, 15

Iron pyrites, 78–79

Jonah, 103

Kalish, Donald, 168 n 14
Kant, Immanuel, 12, 153
Kaplan, David, 145, 169 n 25
Kepler, Johannes, 32, 36
Knowers, idealized, 65
Knowing who, 91–92
Knowledge, 63
Knowledge by description, 95
Kripke, Saul, xvi, xx, 6, 10–11, 17, 42–65 passim, 66–67, 69–92 passim, 102–4, 107–9
  on necessity of identity, 141–42
  semantics for modal logic, 130–37

Language, natural. *See* Ordinary language
Language, perfect, 94
Lesniewski, Stanislaw, 155
Lewis, C.I., 131
Liar paradox, and quotation, 164–66
Logic
  extensional, 29, 50, 54
  free, 24–25
    definite descriptions in, 26
    proper names in, 26
  intensional, 57
  intuitionist, 154
  of knowledge and belief, 65
Logical form, 15, 40
Logical positivists, 92

M, 131, 136
Marcus, Ruth B., 137, 145, 155–56, 158, 165. *See also* Barcan, Ruth
Mars, 80–81
Mary, the Virgin, 55
Mayor of Rome, 91
Meaning, 7–8, 75

Index

Index